Flourishing in Ministry

Flourishing in Ministry

*How to Cultivate
Clergy Wellbeing*

Matt Bloom

An Alban Institute Book

ROWMAN & LITTLEFIELD
Lanham • Boulder • New York • London

Published by Rowman & Littlefield
An imprint of The Rowman & Littlefield Publishing Group, Inc.
4501 Forbes Boulevard, Suite 200, Lanham, Maryland 20706
https://rowman.com

6 Tinworth Street, London SE11 5AL, United Kingdom

British Library Cataloguing in Publication Information Available

Library of Congress Cataloging-in-Publication Data

Includes bibliographic references and index.
ISBN 978-1-5381-1895-5 (cloth : alk. paper)
ISBN 978-1-5381-1896-2 (pbk. : alk. paper)
ISBN 978-1-5381-1897-9 (Electronic)

♾ ™ The paper used in this publication meets the minimum requirements of American National Standard for Information Sciences Permanence of Paper for Printed Library Materials, ANSI/NISO Z39.48-1992.

Contents

Acknowledgments

The Flourishing in Ministry research project has been supported since 2009 by the Lilly Endowment, Inc. I am grateful for the financial resources that Lilly has provided and also for the many opportunities for my team and I to share our research insights with groups of clergy and religious leaders. I am especially thankful to Chris Coble, Jessicah Duckworth, and Craig Dykstra; your support has, in the truest sense, made all of this possible.

The Flourishing in Ministry project is a team of fantastic people. The core team consists of Chris Adams, Kim Bloom, Manuela Casti-Yeagely, Linda Kawental, Sarah Rompola Klinedinst, Judy Miller, and Laura Schmucker. Each of you has played a very important and special role in everything we have accomplished, including this book. And you have supported me in so many ways. I could not have done this book without you. Thank you, team!

The team and I want to thank our great research assistants: Katie Comeau, Gregory Corning, Sophia Costanzo, Emily Degan, Samantha Lessen, Matt Mottern, Letty Ntini, Cary Palmer, Hind Ourahuo, Daniel Pedroza, Bekki Rumschlag, Kathleen Roe, Jackie Rose, Maggie Schmid, Madison Schmucker, James Walutes, and Fer Zambrano. We enjoyed working with each of you. Thanks for filling our office with joy.

And thanks to Kim Brennan, Bethany Cockburn, John Nagy, and Jackie Tachman. We want to recognize you for the contributions you have made to our project and offer our gratitude for your good work.

Thanks to the Collegeville Institute for the many ways you helped me learn how to write. Thank you to the scholars in the Vocations Across to the Lifespan Seminar who welcomed me into their community and became my friends: Laura Kelly Fanucci, Jack Fortin, Joyce Ann Mercer, Bonnie Miller-McLemore, John Neafsey, Jane Patterson, and Katherine Turpin. Thank you to Don Ottenhoff for the wonderful opportunities to learn about writing.

Acknowledgments

Thanks to Michael McGregor for helping me learn how to claim that I am a writer. A special thanks to Kathleen Cahalan; your kindness, encouragement, and wise counsel have been a blessing to me.

Thank you to the staff at Rowman & Littlefield who have helped make this book possible.

To my family: It is hard to find adequate words to express how much you mean to me and to describe the many ways your love inspires and sustains me. Steve Bloom, my brother, you have always believed that I should write a book, and you have continued to champion my work and my writing. Chuck and Mary, my parents, and Nicholas, Keaton, and Maíra, my children: I love you all.

Most of all, to the love of my life, Kim Bloom. For your love, for everything you are, and for everything you have done for me. IHA2.

Finally, on behalf of the Flourishing in Ministry team, I want to thank all of the pastors and clergy who have participated in our research. Our greatest hope is that this book will help you to truly flourish in the important ministry work you do.

Introduction

When I was a child my family worshiped most of the time at a Methodist church. The pastor was Dr. McClure—he was never called "reverend" or "pastor," at least as far as I could tell. For me, he was a dark-robed figure who was always up front and somehow also always "up there," a person to be revered, and so as a child that meant he was also feared a little. On Sunday mornings, he was a voice I barely listened to because I was spending most of my time trying to maximize the small amount of white space in the bulletin to fill with my pictures. One particular Sunday, as my parents were trying to guide my three siblings and me out the door, we were surprised by the smiling face of Dr. McClure, who seemed to appear suddenly, magically before us. I was as dumbfounded as my siblings appeared to be. He spoke to the four kids—I have no idea what he said—and none of us responded. To fill the awkward silence, my mother, perhaps a bit concerned, said to all of us, "You all know who this is, don't you?" I did but was not about to say anything. One of my younger brothers, nodding his head in awe, had an answer. "Yes," he said slowly and reverently, "It's God!"

Certainly, during my childhood, Dr. McClure did represent much of what I understood about God. So, too, did the kindly Reverend Knowles, whose gentle voice, soft hands, and sincere kindness I still remember vividly. I also remember the pastor at the Mennonite church we often attended. He wore a coat and tie in place of a robe, but I knew he was important and kind and yet still mysterious in ways I associated with very religious people. Since those early years I have met many more pastors, and with a few exceptions, most of them have a certain character that I find hard to describe without using words that denote something akin to holy or sacred. Even as I write this, I know that these same men and women would balk at my use of such terms to describe them. To be sure, these are real people who are flawed and wonderful and sinful and marvelous, just like the rest of us. They have their own darker sides, and they would be adamant about describing their "ten thousand faults, foibles, and follies," as one pastor put it. And yet it is these very real and quite amazing people who fill this challenging, difficult, exasperating, but essentially important role of pastor.

Pastoral work is complex, challenging, often arduous, sometimes exhausting, and almost always very important for the lives of church members and communities. In his seminal book on the state of pastoral leadership, Jack Carroll (2006) describes the work of clergy this way:

> Being a pastor is a tough, demanding job, one that is not always very well understood or appreciated. Pastoral work is more complex than that which transpires in the hour or so a week that many lay people see the pastor in action as she or he leads worship and preaches. What happens during this time is surely of central importance to clergy and their parishioners, but it is not the only important thing clergy do. . . . [Moreover,] it is a job in flux. . . . It is made increasingly difficult by rapid changes in the pastor's work environment, including the broader culture in which pastoral work is done.

Other scholars agree. Dr. Richard DeShon (DeShon and Quinn 2007), a leading expert on job analysis—a scientific way of evaluating the responsibilities and activities of jobs—evaluated the role of local church pastors for one Mainline denomination. Dr. Deshon (2010) has studied many professional jobs, and when he finished analyzing the job of local church pastor, he concluded that "the breadth of tasks performed by local church pastors coupled with the rapid switching between task clusters and roles in this position is unique. I have never encountered such a fast-paced job with such varied and impactful responsibilities." Given the strong similarities in pastoral work across denominations, I am confident this description applies to almost all local church pastors. Clergy engaged in "extension" work, those whose ministries are outside of a local church context, usually fill similarly complex and challenging roles. One of the pastors I interviewed, a fifty-year veteran of the craft, told me, "Things are a lot harder for pastors these days. I pray for new pastors—they face things I never even had to think about. It isn't easy being a pastor today."

This tough and demanding work may also be increasingly harmful for pastors. The Duke Clergy Health Initiative, a study of physical and mental wellness of clergy, finds that United Methodist pastors are substantially less healthy than their nonclergy peers. Again, given the similarities in clergy roles across institutions, I would expect to find similar results in other denominations. A study lead by Chris Adams (Adams et al. 2007), a member of our Flourishing in Ministry research team, found that most clergy experience levels of burnout that are higher than most working American. Adams and his colleagues found that clergy are faring better than emergency personnel and police officers when it comes to burnout but are worse off than social workers. Even at moderate levels, burnout is a harbinger of darker things: mental breakdowns, physical collapse, even self-harm. Pastoral work is not only tough; it also may be dangerous.

Even as the work pastors do continues to change and become more challenging and perhaps even dangerous, it is clear that pastors, the social roles they fill, and the work they do continue to be of immense value for hundreds of thousands of people and thousands of churches. Although recent polls indicate religiosity might be waning in the United States, more than 80 percent of Americans still self-describe as religious, and almost 71 percent are still affiliated with a Christian denomination (Pew Forums 2016). When people make decisions about which church to attend, the top two most important criteria are the quality of sermons and how welcoming pastoral leaders are. In other words, pastors still matter, and they matter a great deal.

All of these data beg an important question: How can we help pastors do this important work with excellence and also survive its demands and rigors? I think a better question is: How can we help pastors not just survive but flourish in their work? I formed the Flourishing in Ministry research project to see if science could provide some answers to those questions. We believe that, when work is good, it will produce goodness of many kinds, including high levels of wellbeing among those who perform it. We also believe that work cannot and must not be defined only by measures of performance, such as effectiveness or efficiency. Certainly performance matters, but we vigorously affirm that to be considered truly "good," work must also enhance the wellbeing of all people and all creation that are affected by it, including those who perform it. The mission of the Flourishing in Ministry project is to understand what constitutes good work for pastors, their families, and the churches these pastors serve. We want to understand how to help pastors flourish in ministry so that they, in turn, can enact flourishing ministries that create flourishing churches.

Our current work is directed toward answering three big research questions. The first question is "What are the signature characteristics of wellbeing for clergy?" We want to know how we can tell whether or not a pastor is flourishing. And we want to be able to measure, with accuracy and fidelity, whether a clergy person has a high or low level of wellbeing. We have answers to this first question. We can describe what flourishing is and we can assess it rigorously. Our approach is holistic and comprehensive. We view wellbeing as comprising a variety of elements, and we want to capture this variety in our research. The first four chapters describe our holistic model of wellbeing.

The second research question is "What factors and conditions foster flourishing, and what factors and conditions impede or diminish it?" We have some answers to this question, as well. We have studied factors and conditions at several levels. We explored how the personal characteristics of clergy are related to their level of wellbeing. For example, we know that women in ministry face many more challenges than do men. We know that the wellbeing of early-service pastors is lower, but so, too, is the wellbeing of longer-service pastors. Being new to ministry poses challenges to wellbeing, but so does staying in ministry a long time. We know that variations in life practices such as sleep quality, frequency of vacations, and engagement in certain spiritual disciplines also matter for pastors' wellbeing.

We study how characteristics of local ministry contexts and denominational systems are related to wellbeing. This includes factors such as church size, the fit between the pastor and the local ministry context, and the nature of relationships between pastors and their congregations. We know that moving from one church to another often leads to dramatic declines in wellbeing. And while we also know that denominations want to support their clergy, many clergy are not receiving that help. Our research can help local churches and denominations close that gap.

One very clear result from our research is that a pastor's identity—his or her sense of him- or herself as a person *and* his or her sense of him- or herself as a pastor—is at the core of pastoral wellbeing. As an analogy, we might think of our hearts as one of the core aspects of our physical health. All of the organs are important, but the heart occupies a central place in our physical health. Our identity is, then, the "heart" of our wellbeing. And so a significant portion of this book is devoted to discussion of research on identities, what they are, and how they occupy a central place in understanding and fostering flourishing in ministry.

Our third research question is "How does the wellbeing of clergy and their families change over a life span?" A major focus here is to map the ebbs and flows of wellbeing over an entire life in ministry and to mark the factors that account for those changes. We want to study how the shape and contours of wellbeing change over time, including such things as why the wellbeing of younger and older pastors is fundamentally different from that of mid-service pastors. This longitudinal approach is regarded among scientists as the "gold standard" for research because it is the only way we can really understand what factors influence and shape wellbeing. There is a lot of speculation about what matters, and a long-term study will provide everyone with the data we all need to know, for sure, what helps pastors to flourish over a lifetime in ministry. This is the big question we have yet to answer.

There are more than ten thousand pastors from more than twenty different denominations who have generously participated in our research. Most have participated in our surveys, and several hundred have met with us for long, in-depth interviews and conversations. Our study covers a range of denominational polities, from congregation-based to hierarchical. We have pastors from a variety of church contexts, ranging across Mainline, evangelical, and

Pentecostal; pastors serving small rural churches to large suburban churches and all combinations in between; pastors serving very new to very old churches; and pastors leading churches with worship styles ranging from traditional to contemporary. While most of our pastors are white males, our data also include female pastors, pastors of color from different racial and ethnic backgrounds, and a very wide range of ages and tenures in pastoral ministry. A significant gap in our research is information on the wellbeing of pastors serving in historically Black denominations. We have some pastors from this group but not enough. We are eager to find ways to encourage and engage pastors who might otherwise not have a voice in research. If you are a clergy or a ministry worker of any kind, we welcome you to join with us in our journey toward flourishing at flourishinginministry.org.

The research that I share in this book was the result of the efforts of an entire team of researchers. I am one member of that team; you can find the names of the other team members listed in the acknowledgments. A dozen undergraduate research assistants also joined the team during their time as students at Notre Dame, and each of these students made important contributions to the research. Throughout the book I refer to "our research" simply to avoid more cumbersome phrases such as "the research my team and I conducted." Whenever I refer to "our research," please remember that it took a team to do this work.

I also want to emphasize that I write as a scientist. The information and views I share in this book are science based. I also recognize the importance of theological perspectives and know that most readers will think about the topics and issues in this book from their own theological views. I commend this approach. Science attempts to describe how the world works. Theologies may do the same, but they take the extra step of describing how the world *should* work. Science itself, properly done, makes no claims about what is true, right, moral, noble, or worthy. When scientists make such claims—as I do in this book—we are moving beyond our scientific data. It is sometimes proper for scientists to draw conclusions about, for example, what will make people healthier or improve the quality of marriages. When we do so, however, we are also employing some framework through which we evaluate goodness, rightness, truth, and so on. We often use scientific evidence to support our views, but I also want to confess that our personal moral judgments also shape those views. If I describe what will make pastors happier—as I will—I am making a claim that happiness is a proper thing for pastors to experience. We scientists are, after all, humans, too, and so there are things that we think are important and good and noble. When I make these claims, I offer scientific evidence to support my views, but I also honor that readers may interpret things differently.

In the pages that follow, I present the major findings that have emerged from our study to date. I share some of the quantitative data—numbers are important for describing some aspects of wellbeing. I also share the voices of real pastors from whom we have learned so much. Although I have been able to select only a few, I have carefully chosen these pastoral voices because they represent the many pastors who are serving in churches across the United States and beyond. I hope that pastors who read this book will find themselves reflected in at least one of these stories. I want to begin with the stories of two pastors—Carolyn and Mark—who appear at several places throughout this book. I use the stories of Carolyn and Mark to illustrate some of the important insights from our research. They also provide more comprehensive life stories so we can better see how wellbeing unfolds and how the different dimensions of wellbeing shape each other.

These are composite narratives; they are based on several pastors who are highly similar in important ways. Composite narratives are a powerful method that researchers use to both represent an entire group of people and protect the anonymity of each individual person. Rigorous composite narratives, like the ones I will share about Carolyn and Mark, have to be accurate representations of real pastors living real lives and leading real ministries. But they must also be adapted to properly protect the identities of the pastors who shared so richly with us about their lives and ministries.

CAROLYN

The first interactions with Carolyn to schedule time to meet for an interview were all by email. The initial formality of finding a time that worked with both schedules gave way to humor and self-revelations about the various activities she had in her life, not just as a local church pastor. By the time Carolyn sat for our interviews, she was familiar to the research associate who was collecting the interview data. Upon meeting in person for the first time, there was an easy verbal exchange between the two women.

From a young age, Carolyn had good feelings about the church. Her grandfather was a pastor. While she didn't know exactly what his job involved, she knew that he found meaning in his work and that he was respected. Carolyn's mother and father were active lay leaders in their local congregation, so she spent many weekends and weeknights "tagging along" with them to church events. She knew the layout of the church and knew where to find toys when she was young and where to hide when she was a teenager. She was baptized as an infant, confirmed as a teenager, and active in youth ministry. The church was an integral part of Carolyn's life. Her identity was shaped by the teachings; her spirit was shaped by the worship and the people.

Even though Carolyn had a positive church experience she did not seriously consider a call to ministry when she began exploring careers. She had seen women in ministry but did not know a female pastor whom she identified with. Her father was a scientist, but he had a strong sense of vocation and making positive contributions in the world. Carolyn was raised believing that, whatever she did for paid or nonpaid work, she would have a vocational orientation. As a young child, she played school (always the teacher), hospital (always the doctor), and camp (always the sports coach), so a helping, people-oriented career was a given. She went off to college to pursue medicine and excelled in her studies. During her sophomore year, she added a theology minor as she had always enjoyed reading and studying scripture. Now she was looking for ways to understand theology as an adult. It turned out that she was flourishing in theology more than science. By her senior year, she abandoned thoughts of medical school and applied to seminary.

Seminary pushed her in formative ways. She wrestled with beliefs that had been instilled in her from a young age, discerning what beliefs fit with her adult self. While seminary had been the obvious next step for Carolyn, she was not sure how she would integrate seminary with a career. She put off a decision about a master of divinity or a master of theological studies as long as she could, holding open the possibility of PhD work and teaching theology. As she prayed and discerned, she felt a pull toward the role of pastor. Somehow being a pastor seemed like a blend of teacher, doctor, and sports coach! She felt suited to the role and could articulate a story of God's voice leading her. People who were important to her affirmed they saw gifts for ministry in her.

Carolyn loved the growth and development she experienced in seminary. In this "bubble" with others who were pursuing theological training, she felt affirmed and inspired to be a pastor. Her seminary was a healthy mix of men and women, which reinforced that being a woman in ministry was common. What was happening outside of seminary was a different experience. Friends from high school and college didn't know what to do with a female pastor in the mix. She longed to be Carolyn the person while also developing as Carolyn the preacher, pastor, and caregiver. Conflict arose within Carolyn and also between these meaningful friendships. Could she have fun with her friends? Why did they view her as the moral authority on everything? She struggled with perfectionism, and now this identity tension caused her to be anxious and withdrawn.

She persevered and graduated from seminary eager to begin actual ministry. Some of her earlier friendships healed, others fell away, and she began ministry as the solo pastor of a rural church. While this first call was an overall positive experience and a time of considerable professional growth, she experienced a different kind of challenge: other women questioning her call to ministry and pastoral authority. This challenge caught Carolyn by surprise. She had not expected this, nor was she prepared with emotional resources to quell the pain this criticism caused. She questioned her call to ministry. Maybe women weren't supposed to be pastors. Perhaps those critics were right and she didn't really have gifts for ministry. The seeds of vocation were planted early in her life, and her call to ministry evolved over time and with experience. These critical voices hurt deeply and caused her tremendous pain. She considered leaving ministry and going back to a medical career, perhaps even trying to get into medical school. After all, she knew more female physicians than female pastors. From her perspective female physicians were more respected than female clergy.

After several months of discernment and conversations with family, friends, mentors, and a spiritual director, Carolyn chose to remain in ministry. She was called, and she was a good pastor. Overall, that first call experience was a time of tremendous growth for Carolyn, including finding her voice as a clergywoman, asserting her pastoral authority in appropriate ways, and helping the congregation to grow in supporting their pastor. She became proficient at leading church meetings; officiating at weddings, funerals, and baptisms; learned how to make financial spreadsheets ("they didn't teach that at seminary!"); and grew to understand the relentlessness of Sundays leading worship. When an opportunity arose to be part of a larger, team-based church, she put her name in for consideration. She longed to collaborate with others in ministry and develop programs for multigenerational formation.

In addition, her family was growing. Being near a larger city for her children was a priority. A larger city also held more work opportunities for her spouse. Being a two-career family required negotiating and sharing household responsibilities. Moving to a larger city would put her closer to other family members who could help with childcare. Carolyn was ready for a change. The days were feeling repetitive, she was bored, and something inside of her was longing for a new experience of her call. Within months she had a new church, new home, and new ministry colleagues.

As a full-time associate pastor at a large church supervising several people on the staff team, Carolyn has gained new skills and grown in her identity as a woman and pastor. The lead pastor says that, while Carolyn's title is associate pastor, she functions as a co-pastor with him. They have a healthy and professional work relationship. They both have young children and have taught the congregation that their pastors are multifaceted: pastors, parents, spouses, community volunteers, pilgrims, disciples, humans. She is flourishing in ministry because she has a positive work context, supportive relationships, emotional intelligence and resources, and a flexible call. While she has learned that ministry is difficult work and some days wonders why she ever followed this path, on the macrolevel she is thriving. In future chapters we learn more about Carolyn and the ways she has found to flourish.

JOHN

John is a tall, physically fit, middle-aged pastor from a southern state. His voice is booming, his body language suggests that he is very confident, and every part of him conveys that he is a leader. He joined the Flourishing in Ministry research project through a prestigious skills development program, nominated for the honor by others who saw in him gifts for church leadership. John is a second-career pastor. His first career was in the army, a career that decorated him with medals, honors, and accolades for his success. He is also a former competitive athlete.

Although John was raised with no religious foundation or language, from a young age, he felt an undeniable call, an all-consuming fire, to be a leader. He was raised in a family that prided itself on accomplishments. His home was traditional, in that his father worked out of the home as a laborer and his mother managed the home and John's four siblings. He pushed against authority as a teenager, which led to tensions with his father. When it was time to leave for college, John was happy to be out on his own. It was this rebellious, ambition-driven personality that drew him to the military. He was attracted to the rigor but also the nobility of serving his country. With no one else to think about but himself, he set out to do great things, hoping to be affirmed as a great person.

While in military school, John had his first experience with religion. As a college freshman, as part of basic training, he was required to meet with a chaplain to offset the rigors and intensity of the training. Not one to share openly or to be vulnerable, he was at first put off with this requirement. Gradually he began to open to the idea of becoming a Christian. Finally, in his last year of undergraduate school, John gave his life to Christ. He says at that time he was an unholy and not very good follower of Jesus.

John graduated from college with honors for his military accomplishments. He also had medals from amateur track competitions and was considering a try for the Olympics. His work career began in a school for boys as the director of admissions. The school had a military focus and he wore military dress to work. Central to his identity was the fact that he was a military guy, and he was enormously proud of the rank and status he had achieved. That burning fire to be a leader that he experienced as a young boy was being lived out in ways he couldn't have imagined back then. Along with this John was married and became a father. Even as he excelled, the surety of a life in military leadership began to feel less certain. He'd achieved some of the highest ranks available to him, yet he longed for deeper connections, for work that had more meaning. John rededicated his life to Jesus, began attending church and reading scripture, and even met some other guys who took him under their wing and mentored him as a man of faith. While he had no background or language to describe what he was experiencing and feeling, he began to sense that there was a shift happening in him—a shift from military leadership to something else. Given John's strong personality he describes this shift as he had been called to do amazing things in the military and now he was being called to do amazing things again, this time for God.

John pursued and received a counseling degree and continued his work at the boys' school. He became more involved in a local church, learned the language of religion, and spoke it with ease. His wife and children were plugged into numerous activities. The local church became central to their lives and their schedules. The boys' school promoted him to principal, and he felt that perhaps this was where he would do amazing things for God.

Sitting in worship one Sunday, he received what he described as a clear call from God to be a pastor. His wife quickly affirmed that she could see John as a pastor. Others also commented positively about this new call. A few people suggested that he would be as good a church leader as he had been a military leader. This is what John was hoping he would be. The challenge for him was to figure out how to bring all of his leadership background into the church. He knew exactly how to be a leader and had proven his capacity for a high-level position. With swagger and confidence, John entered seminary.

In seminary he loved studying theology, did well, and graduated on time. He was appointed to a small church, where he was the only pastor, and he unleashed his military leadership and management style on this small group of people. He barked orders and recruited for ministry positions in the same manner that he managed subordinates in the military; he had no patience for discussion and no concept of volunteerism, considered himself to be the last word on any subject, and organized the church in the same hierarchical system he had been steeped in—top-down leadership. It was all he knew.

As you can imagine, things didn't go well for John. He butted heads with nearly everyone in the congregation. All of his formation and training had reinforced a masculine style of leading that career is everything, and that, as the loudest and deepest voice in the room, he was the one in charge.

As we learn in future chapters, John's pastoral identity needed to be formed. Everything in his world was different. If he wanted to be the pastor of a church, he would need to develop different parts of his identity, and he would especially need to learn how to be self-aware. These proved to be difficult experiences for John, his family, and his congregation.

Chapter One

Daily Wellbeing

We hold these truths to be self-evident, that all men are created equal, that all men are endowed by their Creator with certain unalienable Rights, that among these are Life, Liberty, and the pursuit of Happiness.
—U.S. Declaration of Independence

There is something ridiculous and even quite indecent in an individual's claim to be happy.
—Malcolm Muggeridge

THE BRIEF INTRODUCTION TO A NEW SCIENCE OF WELLBEING

Scientists have been actively studying wellbeing for about three decades—only a short time in science years. When I first began my studies of wellbeing nearly twenty years ago, I joined a rapidly growing group of researchers interested in understanding the positive dimensions of human life. My interest arose from my core life values: I believe in the intrinsic value of all human life and I believe that human wellbeing is an intrinsic good. That is, I believe human wellbeing is good in and of itself. I value wellbeing not for what it can lead to (although it can lead to many good things), but rather I believe all people should be able to flourish. The research that my team and I conduct is part of the field of positive psychology, which originated when a group of psychology researchers called for a new science that would help improve human lives. Psychologists have done a lot to help people suffering from depression, anxiety, and many other psychological challenges. Now we have turned our research attention toward helping people achieve wellbeing.

A quick clarification about the terms "wellbeing" and "wellness." Wellness is typically used for our physical health, while wellbeing is used for our psychological, social, and spiritual health. Wellness is about a healthy body and mind; wellbeing is about a flourishing life. Wellness and physical health provide a nice starting place for understanding wellbeing. Our wellness, for example, comprises a number of different dimensions including cardiovascular health, respiratory health, musculoskeletal health, and digestive health. Each of these wellness dimensions has particular health-related capacities. Cardiovascular health, for example, comprises our capacity to rapidly move oxygen, carbon dioxide, nutrients, hormones, and other important materials efficiently throughout our bodies. Our respiratory health is our capacity to bring sufficient oxygen into and remove carbon dioxide from our bodies. Our musculoskeletal health is the body's capacity to move and its ability to provide physical space and protection for all of the other health systems. Our overall wellness, then, is composed of the healthiness of these major dimensions or health systems. When we think about maintaining wellness we know there are complex connections among these major health systems. For example, when we engage in physical exercise, we not only strengthen our muscles and bones but also our cardiovascular and respiratory systems. In turn, healthier cardiovascular and respiratory systems increase the health of our muscles and bones, as well as the health of our brains and other organs. These are just a few of the many important interconnections that work together to create our overall physical health.

We find that a very helpful way to think about wellbeing is to break it into four principle dimensions:

- Daily Wellbeing—the quality of our daily lives.
- Resilience—our capacity to adapt, change, and respond to life's challenges and also our capacity to grow, learn, and develop new capabilities and capacities.
- Authenticity—our sense of self-integrity and dignity.
- Thriving—the meaning and significance we experience in our lives; our sense of having values and beliefs that inspire us, create purpose, and provide moral guidance to our lives; experiencing deep and positive connections with others.

There are smaller subcomponents that make up each of these dimensions, but dealing with those details is often confusing and unhelpful. We find that these four dimensions are a useful way of summarizing the various subcomponents of wellbeing into a framework that we can put to use in our lives. We flourish when we experience daily wellbeing, resilience, self-integrity, and thriving. In the pages ahead, I provide a richer description of each of these building blocks.

Another way to think of these is as four "building blocks of wellbeing" because our wellbeing is an aggregate of four dimensions. There are important interconnections among the building blocks. In fact, they build on each other, so when one dimension goes up, it tends to boost or build up the others. Unfortunately, the reverse is also true: weakening in one building block tends to cause declines in the others. I describe how these interconnections among dimensions are important for restoring and sustaining wellbeing. We need sufficient wellbeing across all four building blocks to experience flourishing.

Conversations about wellbeing often center on the importance of self-care. I find this term troubling because it is often used in ways that seem to overlook or ignore the profound ways our health and wellbeing are impacted by the people and groups we live and work with. There are certainly important responsibilities each of us has for our own wellbeing, but there are also important responsibilities each of us has for each other's wellbeing. We all live in ecosystems of wellbeing. The people we live and work with are part of our ecosystem, but so, too, are the groups and organizations that create and shape the environments in which we live and work. Our wellbeing is shaped by, for example, the health and vitality of our family, co-workers, neighbors, and friends. The contexts in which we live and work are important, as are the organizations in which we participate or are members. Some people live in contexts that constantly undermine their wellbeing. Contexts in which people are ostracized and marginalized, for example, are extremely hostile for wellbeing. Ecosystems of wellbeing figure prominently throughout this book.

As I describe each building block of wellbeing, I highlight both the individual and social aspects of each dimension. It will be important to keep ecosystems of wellbeing in mind. I begin with the dimension of wellbeing that has been the focus of the most research: daily wellbeing, or what scientists often refer to as happiness. I think a happy start to our journey through wellbeing is a good start.

Happiness and Daily Wellbeing

People have probably always been interested in the topic of happiness. Historian Darrin McMahon (2005) notes that one of the first books ever written discusses happiness. But as the epigraphs to this chapter illustrate, and Professor McMahon confirms, happiness has always been a contested idea. Throughout history some people have viewed the pursuit of happiness as the "highest human calling, the most perfect human state," as Thomas Jefferson did, while others, like Muggeridge, have maintained that pursuing happiness is a sure road to ruin and despair. Theologians also seem to disagree about whether happiness is good for humans or not. For example, a 2011 colloquium at the Yale Center for Faith and Culture explored different theological understandings of happiness and human flourishing. I suspect that many of these differences in viewpoints arise from different definitions of happiness.

In this chapter I describe how scientists understand happiness, which is really about daily wellbeing and the quality of day-to-day life. I then share insights from our research about some of the factors that are important for the daily wellbeing of pastors and other people in ministry.

Happiness is used by researchers as an umbrella term that refers to the quality of our daily lives (Diener and Biswas-Diener 2011). More specifically, happiness, or daily wellbeing, is made up of three things: (1) experiencing on a day-to-day basis frequent positive emotions and (2) infrequent negative emotions and (3) having generally positive evaluations about the quality of one's life. Positive emotion comes in many different forms including peacefulness, contentment, compassion, cheerfulness, curiosity, generosity, enthusiasm, wonder, love, and joy. Similarly, there are different kinds of negative emotions including boredom, irritation, frustration, worry, fear, anger, grief, hatred, and sadness. Stress is, unfortunately, a very common negative or unhappy emotion. The third element of daily wellbeing—generally positive evaluations of one's life—is simply how we summarize the quality of our lives. Do we think things in our lives are going well and moving in the right direction, or do we feel our lives are dominated by struggle, pain, and suffering?

The basic idea from science is that our daily wellbeing is higher when we experience more positive feelings than negative feelings and when we think things are, for the most part, going well in our lives (Fredrickson and Losada 2005). I often refer to high daily wellbeing as having more good days than bad days. Research has consistently shown that higher daily wellbeing—having more good, happy days than bad, unhappy days—is essential for our long-term health and growth (Kahneman, Diener, and Schwarz 2003; Lyubomirsky 2008). Dozens of studies have shown that higher daily wellbeing leads to better views of self and others, greater health, less conflict in life, a greater propensity to be helpful to others, better decision making, higher performance in almost any endeavor, greater creativity, and increased capacity to form and sustain positive relationships (Lyubomirsky, King, and Diener 2005; Pressman and Cohen 2005).

Research on daily wellbeing also emphasizes that not all positive feelings are created equal, and neither are all negative feelings (Fredrickson 2004). Some positive feelings, like schadenfreude—delighting in the misfortune of others—are clearly bad for us and for other people. We can also experience artificial happiness when we chase pleasure or when we use drugs or alcohol to create positive feelings. Studies show that pursuing pleasure can have very detrimental effects on our long-term wellbeing. For example, pleasure seeking causes us to make bad health choices and undermines our relationships with others. Pleasure seeking also numbs our long-term capacity to have good days. Like a thrill seeker, we need the next extraordinary "high" to feel even the smallest degree of happiness. But science also shows that some positive feelings like peacefulness, contentment, joy, and love are truly good for us and for the people we interact with. Because we cannot manufacture these truly good feelings—we cannot fake love or joy—they are often referred to as authentic happiness. Experiences of awe and wonder, for example, help us feel connected to something bigger and more important than ourselves and makes us more altruistic, generous, and compassionate (Rudd, Vohs, and Aaker 2012; Stellar et al. 2018). Awe and wonder are powerfully uplifting and can help people overcome challenges and difficulties in life.

Similarly, some negative feelings are important: fear when we face danger, anger over an injustice, guilt over a wrong we have committed, and grief when someone dies. These feelings can motivate us to take action, inspire us to overcome obstacles, lead us to positive personal change, and encourage us to cherish the sanctity of life. Others, like hate, spite, or rage, almost always lead to bad outcomes unless they are carefully controlled. Still others, like frustration, stress, worry, and anxiety, are signals that something is wrong, something that we need to deal with effectively. Research on daily wellbeing seeks to understand how to help people respond well to negative emotions.

Research also shows that daily wellbeing accumulates, but we may be unaware of that impact (Diener and Biswas-Diener 2011). Here is a quick experiment to illustrate this point. Can you remember what you had for lunch yesterday? Most of us probably can. How about a week ago? A month ago? Most of us probably cannot. The flow of our daily lives tends to fade into memory in the same way. We just do not remember the details of our daily lives, but nevertheless those days add up. Good days, and bad days, add up over time and affect our health, our capacity to be at our best, our ability to adapt and change, and a host of other important life outcomes.

Someone once described that being a pastor can sometimes feel like "death by a thousand paper cuts." The point he was making was that pastoral work is challenging and difficult. Pastors are often face to face with human suffering. Their days are long and their workload is heavy. Their work days can sometimes be full of the unhappy experiences of others. Yet pastors often overlook these daily experiences—they are focused on caring for others, not themselves. Science shows that these negative experiences may be piling up. Again, stress is a prime example. The pile of negative experiences gets bigger as one difficult day follows another. As a consequence, their health declines, their decision making suffers, and they are less effective in their work and less capable of dealing with challenges and difficulties. When the pile gets too big, it collapses on them. This is when exhaustion and burnout set in. Happiness research shows us that we need to pay attention to how our days are piling up. Is your pile of unhappy days getting larger? Do you feel like the weeks and months of your life are rushing by? If you feel this way, then step back from the rush of life and pay attention to your everyday experience.

The key insight from all of this research is that we are better off when our typical day-to-day experience is tipped toward daily wellbeing, which includes having more experiences of authentic happiness rather than unhappiness. Science does not advocate for us to try to eliminate all unhappy feelings, but rather it alerts us to pay attention to the negative feelings we experience and find ways to respond well to them. Ignoring stress, for example, will not work. The better approach is to reduce or eliminate sources of stress when we can and learn how to cope effectively with the stress we cannot eliminate.

Daily Wellbeing among Clergy

How are pastors doing with their daily wellbeing? Our survey data indicate that 80 percent of men and women in pastoral ministry are satisfied and very engaged with their ministry job. Similarly, 80 percent of clergy, both men and women, report high levels of general happiness. Of course, this means that a significant portion—about 20 percent of both men and women—are dissatisfied with their ministry job and feel frustrated or disengaged from their pastoral work. So while the good news is that most pastors report being happy and satisfied with their ministry work, those who struggle with their day-to-day ministry life seem to face very significant challenges.

When we move to survey results on daily wellbeing, the results are more troubling. Almost 40 percent of all clergy report low satisfaction with their overall life. For both men and women, 38 percent report significant deficits in their daily wellbeing outside of ministry. And slightly more than 40 percent—41 percent of women and 42 percent of men—report high levels of daily stress. We asked about their overall experience of stress in our surveys, so we do not know how much of this stress is related to ministry work and how much is related to other factors.

These data present an interesting paradox: most clergy report being very satisfied and engaged with their ministry work and also being generally happy, but many of these clergy also report experiencing significant daily stress and feeling dissatisfied with their overall lives. I want to exhort against drawing conclusions about what might explain this paradox. I have heard several conclusions—pastors are deceiving themselves into believing they are satisfied with ministry, pastors love their work too much, pastors overinvest in work and underinvest in the rest of their lives—and these explanations may, at most, offer a partial explanation. We do not fully understand the dynamics underlying clergies' daily wellbeing, and there is more we need to learn.

When we combine data from our interview studies with these survey results, we can begin to gain insights into these seemingly paradoxical results. I think that half of all pastors are doing well on all aspects of daily wellbeing. That is, they are satisfied with both their work and their overall lives. They are generally happy and experience low to moderate amounts of stress. So about half of pastors are doing very well with daily wellbeing. They are authentically happy in their ministry and in life.

Nearly a quarter of pastors, however, find daily life very challenging, both in their ministry work and in their lives outside of ministry. These pastors are clearly in difficult and dangerous wellbeing territory. As I describe in the next chapter, they are almost certainly burned out, and they may be suffering from declines in their physical health, as well. These are the walking wounded of pastoral ministry; they are trying to carry on in spite of their very low daily wellbeing. These pastors are also the most likely to express a desire to leave ministry: they need help to find a way forward, and when help is hard to find, they look for a way to get out. These pastors often experience shame and guilt; they blame themselves for their predicament, which makes asking for help even more difficult. And many worry that if their condition becomes known by others, they will lose their job—"it's probably better to quit than to get fired," as one pastor with very low daily wellbeing told us. And so they press on, hoping things will get better. Things rarely get better for these pastors because they are in a downward spiral in which low daily wellbeing begins to erode their resilience and eventually causes declines in the other dimensions of wellbeing. In the final chapter, I describe ways that local churches and denominations can help pastors flourish, and responding to pastors in this group is an important task for both groups.

Another 25 percent of pastors are sliding downward and risk joining the ranks of the walking wounded of pastoral ministry. These pastors would benefit, perhaps a great deal, from adopting one or two of the "small step" wellbeing practices I describe in the last chapter. We call these small steps because they do not take very much time—five to ten minutes a day—yet when practiced regularly, they can lead to significant boosts in daily wellbeing. For example, spending a few minutes in centering or contemplative prayer will help. Another small step is to end the work day on a high note. A high-note ministry activity is something that a pastor both enjoys and can do well. These activities can create something like a flow experience—a positive moment of doing something that is important, doing it well, and enjoying the experience of engaging in that activity. There are some kinds of enjoyment that boost our daily wellbeing and therefore, I argue, are good for us to experience. There are enough small-step practices that there is something that will work for all pastors.

There is much more we need to understand about daily wellbeing among pastors and to fully explain the paradox our research has revealed. One key is that we need to learn more about pastors' day-to-day experiences. Surveys gather information at one point in time and require that pastors summarize their overall experiences to answer a few questions. Daily life studies provide information on the ebbs and flows of daily wellbeing and produce insights about what causes those changes. We need this richer and more nuanced information to identify the root causes of the daily struggles that so many pastors face, as well as the wellsprings of joy in ministry that many others are blessed to experience.

A Theology of Happiness and Daily Wellbeing?

I find that the term "happiness" is a fraught concept for some pastors. "I was called to serve, not to be happy" is the kind of refrain I have heard from these pastors. Some pastors and senior pastoral leaders have told me that happiness is not even a theological term; others have said that the Bible warns us against happiness. But others see happiness as a vital part of Christian life. John Wesley, for example, believed that the essence of the Christian experience was "happiness and holiness," which he contrasted with worldly happiness (Clapper 2011). We were clearly created to feel positive moods and emotions—delight, joy, peace, wonder, excitement, and, yes, also pleasure and passion. While social science can describe something about the causes and consequences of happiness, it offers no guidance about when and why these kinds of moods and emotions are morally good for us, and it has little to say about when and why they will lead us astray. We need theological perspectives to deepen and sharpen our understanding of wellbeing, particularly happiness. Theologies can, for example, help us avoid the traps of worldly happiness and also guide us toward finding authentic happiness. Theologies can help us understand the renewing, perhaps even redemptive, power of positive feelings. Researchers have recently begun to focus on experiences of awe and wonder, and studies show these positive experiences can enhance wellbeing (Bai et al. 2017; Rudd, Vohs, and Aaker 2012; Stellar et al. 2018). Some of the most exciting research, at least in my view, is showing how experiences of awe foster humility and encourage prosocial behavior. There is much that science can learn from theological perspectives about what kinds of happy, positive experiences we should seek for ourselves and for others.

PASTOR-MINISTRY ALIGNMENT

Researchers have long emphasized that a good "fit" or alignment between people and their work environment is necessary for them to perform well and to be satisfied in their work. This is true for pastors, as well. In broad terms, pastor-ministry alignment refers to the compatibility between a pastor and the ministry context in which the pastor serves. There are several important kinds of pastor-ministry alignment, and our research results consistently show that each form of alignment is a crucial factor in daily wellbeing and ministry effectiveness.

Competencies-Duties Alignment

The first is competencies-duties alignment, which refers to whether a pastor has the knowledge, skills, abilities, and experience needed to undertake the duties of the particular pastoral role the pastor currently fills. Can the pastor preach in the specific style that works best at his or her current church? Does the pastor have the capacity to lead the other pastors, staff, and volunteers at his or her church? Is the pastor skillful in providing the kinds of pastoral care needed by the members of his or her church? Is the pastor skilled at managing the unique outreach programs that are a central part of the ministry of his or her church? Clearly then, in addition to being important for clergy wellbeing, good competencies-duties alignment is essential for pastoral effectiveness.

Typically, pastors have most of the competencies needed but find they lack the right knowledge, skills, or abilities for one or a few ministry duties. In fact, it is rare for a pastor to have all of the competencies needed for a particular pastoral role. Dr. Richard DeShon, a professor at Michigan State University, is an expert in job analysis, a sophisticated research methodology for systematically analyzing the tasks, activities, and responsibilities of a particular job. He and a colleague (DeShon and Quinn 2007) conducted an analysis of the "job" of a local church pastor and concluded that he has "never encountered" a job that is as complex, varied, and impactful as the work of local church pastors. In a follow-up study, Dr. Deshon (2010) determined that performing all of the tasks required of most local church pastors would require sixty-four different personal competencies. This led him to also conclude that "it is almost inconceivable to imagine that a single person could be uniformly high on the sixty-four distinct knowledge, skills, abilities, and personal characteristics."

The challenge for many pastors is that they think they must have all sixty-four competencies needed to perform every duty and responsibility of their pastoral role. One pastor we interviewed put this well when he said, "When we are called to ministry, we are called to be excellent, not mediocre." Many pastors echoed this sentiment that they wanted to be able to perform all of their ministry duties and responsibilities with a high level of excellence. Often the members of their church also expect that the pastor can do it all and do it all well. Judicatories and denominations also often seem to act on the same expectation that every pastor has all sixty-four competencies. And if the pastor does not, then the typical response is "The pastor needs to ask for help." There is truth in that assertion, but it is also true that there should be a similar expectation on lay leaders, church members, and judicatory leaders to offer help to pastors. My experience is that pastors are held responsible for either having the competencies or ensuring they get the help of someone who does. A better scenario would be one in which pastors do seek help *and* others offer the help.

The importance of competencies-duties alignment for both pastoral well-being and ministry effectiveness also points to the importance of having very effective ways to select or appoint pastors to ministry roles. Again, my experience with the appointment/call processes used by several different denominations is that there is significant room for improvement. One major area for improvement would be to have lay leaders and judicatory leaders (an outside perspective would be crucially important) conduct a candid and comprehensive assessment of the church's ministry strengths and weaknesses, as well as the church's ministry hopes and aspirations. This assessment could be augmented by an assessment of the competencies available among the members. Similarly, pastors should do a candid assessment of their own competencies, noting which of the sixty-four they have at a full level and which of the sixty-four they lack. An outsider's assessment of pastoral competencies would also be important. A much better match could be made with this kind of information about both the church and the pastor. Competencies-duties alignment would be higher, pastors would be more effective, and they would be more likely to flourish.

Needs-Supplies Alignment

Needs-supplies is a second form of alignment that refers to the degree to which a particular pastoral role supplies the resources required to meet the needs of a pastor and the pastor's family. Does the church provide appropriate professional development opportunities for the pastor? Are the compensation and benefits adequate? Does the local church provide sufficient time away from work for the pastor? Are work duties scheduled in a way that is sensitive to the pastor's family life? Needs-supplies alignment is often overlooked. Pastors are reluctant to raise concerns with lay leaders when there is misalignment between needs and supplies. (When speaking about time away for rest, one pastor said he had "days off-ish.") Lay leaders may also be reluctant to raise concerns, especially if the church has limited resources. The worst situations are those in which the local church is insensitive or antagonistic to the needs of pastors and their families. We have heard stories of pastors being required to live in parsonages ravaged by mold or without working bathrooms. We have also heard stories of churches spending money on favorite ministry programs instead of providing adequate pay and benefits to their pastors. These are examples of poor needs-supplies alignment. These are all-too-common examples.

Beginning in 2015, the Lilly Endowment, Inc. supported more than 110 initiatives at a wide range of denominations and seminaries to explore and address the economic challenges facing pastors. We have conducted our own studies of personal financial issues and how they impact clergy wellbeing. A consistent finding across the various Lilly-funded initiatives and our research is that a significant portion of clergy—one-third in many denominations—face significant financial challenges that are caused by high seminary debt and salaries that are insufficient for monthly living needs and often inadequate for future needs such as emergencies and the education of the pastor's children. In addition, an increasing number of pastors have no health, life, or disability insurance. Many of these pastors are reluctant to discuss financial issues with the lay leaders at their churches, and it appears that lay leaders rarely initiate those conversations with pastors. Conversations about money are fraught with theological uncertainties. Several pastors we interviewed wondered if "I should just be grateful for whatever gifts God provides to me as a pastor," even as they admitted it was hard for them to cover their families' living expenses. We have also heard stories of local churches that refuse to pay their pastors a sufficient salary, and, of course there are churches that simply cannot pay their pastors enough. Judicatories and denominations are sometimes silent partners to this insidious problem, leaving it to pastors and lay leaders to figure out how to solve any needs-supplies problems. Furthermore, within most denominations, pastor salaries and benefits differ significantly from church to church, so a new call or appointment can bring with it a dramatic change in the pastor's financial condition. Again, solving these problems is often left to the pastor.

The pastor pay problem is thorny, complicated, and loaded with strong emotions. It is a secret problem that is hidden in plain sight: everyone knows it is a problem, but few people appear willing to acknowledge and address it. But the consequences of poor needs-supplies alignment can be dire. Left unaddressed, poor needs-supplies alignment creates significant work stress, as pastors struggle to continue working hard without appropriate pay or benefits. Pastors take on credit card debt to close the gap between their salaries and the living needs of their families. On top of the seminary loans that many of these pastors carry, their debt load increases each month. To increase their monthly take-home pay, an alarming number of pastors are foregoing Social Security tax payments, which puts their retirement incomes in jeopardy.

If local church leaders do not respond, pastors may experience a compromised sense of respect and care from their church members. Pastoral effectiveness can be diminished as financial worries and work stressors build. Poor needs-supplies alignment can spill over to life outside of ministry. It is a source of work-family strain and can be a potent source of marital stress between pastor and spouse.

Values Alignment

The match among a pastor's core life values, religious beliefs, and fundamental orientation to ministry and those of the church the pastor is serving is
values alignment. Another way of thinking about values alignment is the
degree to which a pastor's theology is similar to the theology of the local
church the pastor leads. I use the term "theology" here to mean the deep
convictions that a pastor holds about what it means to be a Christian, what
kind of life Christians are called to lead, and the role that a local church is
called to fill in the world. Churches also have their own theologies about
what it means to be a Christian, live a Christian life, and be a church that
fulfills God's will.

Values alignment goes deeper than agreement between the pastor and lay
leaders about certain ministry programs, and it is deeper than differences
between those with more conservative and those with more progressive beliefs. Strong alignment reflects deep agreement about the essentials of a life
of faith. Certainly this deep agreement (or disagreement in the case of values
misalignment) can be, and often is, made clearest around important social
issues. Values alignment (or misalignment) also becomes more concrete in
actions that reflect understandings about the essential role of the church in
the world. Many of the younger pastors we have interviewed have a deep
belief that the vital work of a local church is "beyond the church's walls,"
and these pastors have a strong commitment to mission work. Yet some of
these pastors find themselves leading churches that have a more inward focus
in which members devote most of their time and resources to ministry programs that serve current members. Certainly, most pastors and churches
would agree that some balance between inward-focused and mission-focused
activities is optimal. What matters for values alignment is what one pastor
referred to as "where the heart and soul of ministry is. . . . Do the church and
I agree about what are the most important things for us, as Christians and as
this church, to do in the world?"

Each of these three forms of alignment is fundamental for both pastoral
effectiveness and pastoral wellbeing. But values alignment is the most important. Pastors who feel very capable of undertaking the ministry duties of
their local churches will not flourish unless they also believe in the importance of those duties. Values alignment matters most because values, beliefs,
and moral convictions are an essential part of a pastor's identity. A pastor's
personal theology animates his or her call to ministry and defines, for that
pastor, what Wayne Oates (1982) calls "work-centered meaning of your
existence as a Christian pastor." In chapter 3 on authenticity, I share more
about the central role that a pastor's identity plays in wellbeing and ministry
effectiveness. What I want to highlight here is that connection between values alignment and pastoral identity. Values misalignment matters because it

is a disagreement about issues of fundamental importance. Values misalignment requires either that a pastor compromise his or her identity or engage in the difficult work of trying to change the theology of a church. The first response results in what researcher Patricia Hewlin (2009) calls "facades of conformity": acting like one agrees with values or beliefs that are, in fact, at odds with one's own values and beliefs. Enacting facades of conformity requires a great deal of mental, emotional, and spiritual energy and, therefore, are very corrosive to wellbeing.

Here again, better values alignment can be facilitated through improvements in the processes used to call or appoint pastors to local churches. An articulation of core values and beliefs by both the prospective pastor and the local church could be a starting place. These "statements of belief" can be catalysts for fruitful discussion between pastor candidates and lay leaders. Candid conversations about areas of agreement and disagreement could help ensure that values alignment is stronger.

Summary of Alignment

At this point in time, our research clearly shows that all three forms of alignment are essential for both pastoral effectiveness and wellbeing. What we do not know is how good (or bad) alignment forms. Does it happen early in a pastor's tenure at a church and never change? Or does alignment emerge over time? (This is the more likely scenario.) Does alignment change? I think it does because pastors change, churches change, and the world around a pastor and a church changes. I think pastors and churches sometimes overlook or misunderstand these changes and consequently overlook misalignment when it is forming. What causes good alignment to form or prevents good alignment from forming? What role does a pastor play in creating alignment? What role does the local church, especially its lay leaders, play in forming alignment? I am certain that alignment, whether good or poor, results from the combined efforts of pastors and churches. When good alignment forms, it is because the pastor and lay leaders have worked together to create a pastoral role that is right for both a particular pastor and a particular church. Our research has already yielded some important insights into how pastors can create better alignment through a process that researchers refer to as "job crafting." These insights also shed light on how churches and lay leaders can foster better alignment.

Job Crafting

Job crafting refers to actions pastors take to change the tasks and activities, social interactions, and work style of the pastoral role they are trying to fill. Some of the tasks, activities, and social interactions are core features of almost any pastoral role—activities such as preaching, leading worship, pastoral care, and teaching are core features. Pastors are able to create better alignment when they "personalize" these core features. Here are illustrative examples of three pastors who were able to personalize their preaching: "I'm not an inspirational guy, so I am more teacher in the pulpit than charismatic preacher"; "I really love stories and storytelling, so that is always a part of my sermons"; and "I don't write out my sermons. I pick a topic and read scripture, and then on Sunday I just let the Spirit flow and fire me up. I just let go, and God does the rest." In each of these examples, preaching was still regarded as an essential feature of the pastoral role, yet each of these pastors was able to personalize his or her approach to preaching. If pastors feel compelled to adopt a style of preaching that is less authentic for them, then alignment in at least this one, crucially important, core role feature is strained. We also found that pastors were able to achieve better alignment when they were able to find church members whose gifts and graces complemented the pastor's. A common example was pastors who partnered with lay leaders to fill in the gaps in the pastor's financial management skills. These pastor-parishioner partnerships were sometimes initiated by the pastor and sometimes by lay leaders. What mattered most was that lay leaders created a supportive environment that made it easier for the pastor to share his or her skill deficits.

Pastors who achieved the best alignment went further in crafting their pastoral role. A pastor with an undergraduate degree in marine biology described herself as a "committed environmentalist." She created an annual sermon series on "caring for God's creation," in which congregants were invited to work in the church's community garden. She has continued to do this sermon series each year, and she has added more environment-oriented ministries that help her church "be more connected to our local community." She describes herself as "a pastor for people and the earth," giving voice to how claiming this peripheral feature helped her experience personal authenticity. Another pastor who was a theater major in college incorporated drama into Sunday worship at his church. Another pastor has a passion for music and provides low- or no-cost music lessons to children in her local community. Other members of her church have joined her and have created a highly effective missions program as a result.

Leadership is a particularly nuanced feature of most pastoral roles. There are a number of popular theories of leadership, including Edwin Friedman's *A Failure of Nerve* (2007) and Ronald Heifetz, Alexander Grashow, and Marty Linsky's *The Practice of Adaptive Leadership* (2009). While many of these theories offer useful ideas that many pastors may find helpful, the essence of effective leadership always arises from crafting a style of leadership that fits with each pastor's unique life history, personality, and talents. Some pastors may find a more charismatic, transformational style is a better fit for them, while other pastors may find they are more effective when they adopt a servant leadership style. To be sure, any leadership style must include certain core leadership activities such as making key decisions, creating a vision, and guiding others as they participate in ministry activities, but there are a variety of ways to undertake each of these core leadership activities.

I find that pastoral leadership is often portrayed as if there were one right way to undertake it. "Effective pastors are innovative" is one of the more common examples of this one right way. I understand why innovation is perceived to be important, especially given the declining membership in American churches. While all pastors can learn tools and techniques for innovation, pastors vary widely in their own capacity to be innovative. I have taught classes on innovation for more than a decade, so I have firsthand experience with a variety of leaders who are trying to become more innovative. While all pastors can learn principles of innovation, only some pastors have the talent required to achieve the kinds of "radical innovation" that create major, positive changes. This is true of leaders in other settings, as well. Many pastors are able to use the principles of innovation to create improvements in ministry activities, which is itself helpful, but radical innovations are beyond their capacities. This does not make these pastors innovation failures—their strongest capacities likely reside in other areas of ministry. Furthermore, "big idea" people tend to lack skill in dealing with details, and they are often poorly organized. This is true of the most innovative pastors: they are often deficient in core ministry areas such as management and administration. My point here is to again emphasize that each pastor has his or her own unique style or approach to being an effective leader—there is no one best way for all pastors to lead. And it is rare that any pastor has all sixty-four competencies (sixty-five if we add innovation to the list).

Chapter Two

Resilience

Karen experienced a call to ministry while she was teaching elementary school after college. Her faith had always been important to her, and she had felt called to ministry earlier in her life, but she had no female clergy examples to help her articulate the call. When she did meet a female pastor, she spent a year in spiritual direction to discern what God was doing in her life. That opened the door for other mentors, and she entered full-time ministry. That was twenty years ago.

Karen speaks positively about her years in ministry, especially the joy of journeying with people through many life transitions. She has flourished in her pastoral positions and expects to be in ministry for another decade. While Karen recounts many lovely stories about pastoral ministry, she also describes difficulties and challenges, including parishioners' demanding expectations, comments about her haircut rather than her sermon, loneliness and isolation, and church commitments six out of seven evenings.

What stands out with Karen is her ability to hold both the highs and lows of ministry together. She admits that sometimes the difficulties seem to pile up, but she's learned to check in with herself about feelings, consider whether she's sleeping and eating enough, or talk to a ministry colleague for perspective. Some of these self-awareness skills she learned as a young adult. One of her mentors early in ministry helped her set boundaries and learn to pay attention to her "spiritual wellspring."

She expects to move in the next year and have a new congregation in a new city, and her youngest child will leave home. Her husband appears to be developing health concerns. There are changes on the horizon for Karen, and she will need to tap into emotional and physical reserves. Fortunately, she has those reserves. Because Karen is resilient, she is able to roll with the highs and lows of life and ministry while keeping an overall positive attitude and hopefulness about the future.

Resilience comprises our capacities to adjust to changes in the world around us, to achieve our life goals, and to keep growing and reaching toward our fullest potential. Wellbeing is not static—it goes with the flow of our lives—and so resilience is, in part, our ability to respond to the changing and sometimes challenging world around us. Resilient people are able to respond effectively to difficulties and crises, and they are not diminished or damaged by such experiences. They may experience temporary declines in their overall wellbeing, but because they are resilient, they can recover quickly. Resilience also comprises our capacities for growth and personal development. Resilient people are able to increase their knowledge and abilities, develop new capabilities, and learn new things. They have an internal drive to learn more about themselves so they can grow as a person.

The opposite of resilience is burnout. Burnout is a dangerous condition because it leads to depression, anxiety, nervous breakdowns, divorce, and even suicide. Burnout is insidious. It sneaks up on people: most burned-out pastors do not realize they are in such a precarious position. Burnout begins with fatigue and progresses to exhaustion. Burned-out pastors feel tired all the time. They may often feel they do not have enough energy for their daily ministry tasks. Sundays, in particular, feel overwhelming. Exhaustion then leads to ineffectiveness. Burned-out people can no longer perform at their best. They find even easy tasks to be challenging and difficult. They notice the declines in their performance, which feeds their exhaustion, making the burnout even worse. Eventually, as exhaustion and ineffectiveness build, burned-out pastors experience despair, detachment, and sometimes cynicism. After this point, things become very dire, as people "crash and burn" or have a "nervous breakdown" (many burned-out pastors use phrases like these). They can no longer continue, so they give up or break down.

Results from our research on resilience and burnout raise some concerns. We find that, across denominations, more than one-third of all pastors (35 percent of women and 38 percent of men) report significant levels of burnout. Some of this is likely due to poor pastor-church alignment, but there are other causes that we must still sort out. Another third of pastors seem to be highly resilient, but most of these are mid-service pastors, meaning they have been in ministry at least seven years. Pastors who are new to ministry seem to be especially prone to burnout, as are some longer-tenured pastors. These results do suggest that one potential cause of early exits from ministry is burnout, but there are most certainly other causes. It is most certainly not the case that every pastor who leaves ministry is burned out. In fact, it appears that a large number leave to find new contexts that are more conducive to their calls to ministry. But these data still highlight the need to address burnout in the early years of ministry. And these data are cause for concern about the resilience of pastors as they retire from active ministry life. We do not have a great deal of research data on these pastors, so there is much we do not know. But the data we have indicate that some of these are likely to be among the walking wounded pastors I described in chapter 1. Transitioning out of ministry is a big change, and pastors need a great deal of resilience to deal with even the best and most positive ministry transitions. These late-service pastors with low resilience will likely need extra support as they move into the next stage of their lives and ministries.

THE ESSENTIAL ELEMENTS OF RESILIENCE

Researchers use the term "self-regulation" to describe three of the essential elements of resilience. There are three self-regulatory capacities: self-awareness, self-reflectivity, and self-control (Diamond 2013). Self-awareness is the ability to step back from the flow of life to notice what we are feeling, thinking, and doing. It is the capacity to pay attention and recognize what is happening inside us and around us. Researchers have discovered that we too often live in a fog, unaware of why we do, say, and feel the things we do. We can often come up with explanations after the fact, but a significant portion of our behavior is beyond our conscious awareness. People with high self-awareness are able to get out of this fog. They have an ongoing ability to notice things like "I am feeling this particular mood or emotion," "I am thinking about this topic," or "I responded to that person in this specific way." When we describe someone as being a "bull in a china shop," we are describing someone with little to no self-awareness. Likewise self-awareness is not self-consciousness, that overly sensitive, uncomfortable form of self-attention many of us experienced during our adolescence, when we thought so much about ourselves we became ill at ease. Self-awareness strikes a Goldilocks place of not too much nor too little self-thinking.

Self-reflectivity is the ability to examine and think about our thoughts, feelings, and behaviors, especially in terms of whether or not they are appropriate, good, helpful, or otherwise positive for ourselves, for other people, and for the world around us. Self-reflectivity builds on self-awareness to gain an understanding of how a particular thought, feeling, or response impacted ourselves and others. Self-awareness provides information about what is happening, and through self-reflectivity we figure out why we responded as we did and determine whether that response led to positive or negative outcomes. Emotional intelligence—the capacity to recognize and understand our emotions and the emotions of others—is one example of how self-awareness and self-reflectivity work together. Self-reflectivity is not ruminating about ourselves, working each thought, feeling, or action into a knotty, messy ball of hyper-self-criticism. Self-reflectivity strikes another Goldilocks place of noticing what is going on inside and around us and what role we have played in those goings-on.

The Serenity Prayer (attributed to Reinhold Niebuhr) is a masterful summary of the third self-regulatory capacity, self-control: "God, give us grace to accept with serenity the things that cannot be changed / Courage to change the things which should be changed / and the Wisdom to distinguish the one from the other." Once self-awareness and self-reflectivity have provided us with the information about what is happening inside and around us and why it is happening, self-control is our capacity to respond to that information. Self-control is our ability to change things in ourselves and the world around us. It includes our ability to set and achieve goals in life, to change things about ourselves (for example, giving up bad habits), and to adapt and adjust to the world around us (for example, learning how to work better with a difficult colleague). It also includes our capacity to change the world around us to make it more suitable for ourselves and others (for example, saying no to another request from our boss to work late). And as Niebuhr's prayer emphasizes, self-control is also our ability to distinguish when we should try to change the world and when we should change ourselves. Self-control is sometimes called willpower or agency. The word "willpower" captures our capacities to control our urges and impulses and our ability to do the right thing even in the face of difficulties. The word "agency" captures our abilities to take action, to think ahead and be proactive, and to set the right goals and persist in achieving them. Setting appropriate boundaries around work and then sticking to those boundaries is an example of high self-control.

Researcher Roy Baumeister (Baumeister and Tierney 2011) uses the "muscle" metaphor to illustrate how self-control works. When we use a muscle it gets tired; rest is required to build back its strength. Similarly, using our self-control temporarily weakens that capacity. If we have to exert a lot of willpower, say to continue working in a very challenging context, our willpower reserves are depleted. This means that a series of bad days will likely weaken our resilience, which, in turn, will diminish our capacity to deal effectively with more bad days. During that low state, even simple problems can become insurmountable. This is when we might, for example, say things we don't mean out of anger or find ourselves unable to face another day of work.

A fourth major element of resilience is positive life dynamics. Life dynamics give shape and form to our lives, and in turn, they shape our daily wellbeing and resilience. They include things like how many activities and responsibilities we have day to day, the patterns and qualities of our regular social interactions, and the high points and stressors that typify our daily lives. Life dynamics tend to endure over time so they have a longer-term effect on our wellbeing. Poor life dynamics create stress. Stress builds up over time because the underlying dynamics that cause it do not change.

Life dynamics form the rhythms of resilience because they create a cadence or pace in our life that shapes our self-regulatory capacities and our daily wellbeing. Positive life dynamics are more regular, smooth, and harmonious. They create more good days than bad days. They boost our resilience. Negative life dynamics are irregular, discordant, and painful. They create stress. They create more bad days and leave little room for good days. They stretch our resilience, sometimes to the breaking point. Sometimes we can adjust to negative life dynamics. Take the experiences of new parents at home with their first baby as an example. The first few days are a chaotic blur, but over time most parents learn to adjust, at least in some ways, to the baby's schedule, and they also help the baby develop a smoother pattern of sleep, feeding, changing, and so on. But in other cases, we cannot control or adjust to the underlying dynamics that are creating stress. In these cases, we need help to turn the negative dynamic into a more positive one.

Work has its dynamics, as well. Workload is one of the most common work dynamics. Workload refers to the amount of work a person has and the pace of his or her work. When someone says "I'm juggling too many things at work" or "I spend all day fighting fires," he or she is describing a workload that has created a stressful dynamic at work. As I will share shortly, workload is one of the most important work and life dynamics for pastors and one of the most overlooked and misunderstood elements of pastoral wellbeing.

A BURDEN TOO HEAVY?

In this section, I share what we have learned about how the work pastors do day by day in a local church shapes their wellbeing. By work I mean what pastors do—the actual tasks, activities, and responsibilities of their work role—and how pastors experience their work. Earlier in this book, I referenced one of the conclusions Jackson Carroll draws from the results of his 2006 study of pastoral leadership, that "being a pastor is a tough, demanding job." Dr. DeShon's research confirms this judgment.

In our 2013 *Emerging Research Insights* (Bloom 2013) report, we arrived at similar conclusions about the work of local church clergy. We noted that pastoral work seems to require expert-*generalists*, people who are highly skilled at performing a wide range of tasks and activities. Most individuals, in fact, are expert-*specialists*: highly skilled to perform some of these tasks, less skilled to perform others, and insufficiently skilled to perform still others. Pastors know this about themselves, and so they understand that the best ministry opportunities are the ones in which their best skills fit or match the ministry context. For example, pastors highly skilled in evangelism are best suited for church planting, those highly skilled in teaching will likely perform best in churches that emphasize learning and study, and pastors highly skilled in caregiving will likely serve most effectively at churches with extensive congregational needs. Yes, some amount of evangelism, teaching, caregiving, and so forth is needed in most ministry contexts, but the relative balance of those performance needs differs regardless of what church boards or denominational leaders assert.

Like Carroll and DeShon, I find that the work requirements of a local church pastor are complex and varied and require a high degree of specialized knowledge and skill. That kind of work is not necessarily bad for wellbeing, and many pastors flourish doing this often tough and demanding work. However, comparing what Carroll found in his research and what we find in ours, it appears that more pastors today are finding their work too tough and demanding. We find that a significant portion of pastors experience high work demands and high levels of work-related stress. Our data also show that a considerable number of pastors report low levels of work-life balance. Perhaps most alarming, we find that over one-third of pastors are experiencing high to severe levels of burnout. These data are clear indicators that some pastors—too many in our view—are overburdened. To be sure, while ministry work can be demanding, it can also be deeply engaging, absorbing, and meaningful. But the very things that make pastoral work so meaningful can also make it extremely taxing. The potential for overinvestments in ministry work are high because it can be difficult for pastors to find the tipping point between positive engagement and oversacrificing, between fatigue due to a ministry job well done and exhaustion due to overinvesting.

THE BURDENS OF MINISTRY WORK

Over the past four years, I have conducted additional research into the workload and work demand of local church pastors and compared those insights with what we learned from the work of physicians, teachers, international aid workers, and global health professionals. There are six characteristics of ministry work that create potential challenges for the wellbeing of clergy. When pastors face work that meets even three of these characteristics, they are facing a workload that will likely undermine their wellbeing. The longer the pastor experiences that workload, the more damaging it will be to his or her wellbeing.

(1) Ministry Is High-Stakes Work

There is a great deal at stake in ministry work. Pastors deal directly with the most important and sacred dimensions of human life. Pastors are responsible for helping people engage in spiritual transformation. Pastors care for people during some of the most difficult and tragic experiences in their lives. Pastors lead spiritual communities toward transforming the world. Pastors must also be effective managers. Most pastors are responsible for running a business in addition to being the spiritual leader of a faith community. Almost all ministry activities carry the potential for making a significant impact, for better or for worse, on the lives of other people. The potential benefits of excellent performance are high, and the mistakes or failures of poor performance can carry heavy costs because so much is at stake in ministry work.

(2) Ministry Work Is Complex, Continuous, and Diverse

Most tasks and activities that pastors are responsible for are *complex*, meaning they require the application of higher-order knowledge, skills, and abilities. Performing complex activities and tasks effectively requires high levels of cognitive effort (concentration, reasoning, problem solving, working memory, inference control, etc.), physical stamina, and emotional control. These kinds of tasks do have a very strong upside. Most pastors like immersing themselves in their work. They appreciate working hard. Most embrace opportunities to take on a ministry challenge. The key issue here is that the mix of ministry work may include few easy tasks, the kind that require less effort. Researchers have found that having some "mindless" work mixed in with complex tasks can boost creativity, and it also has positive benefits on wellbeing because, for example, it creates "microbreaks" in the middle of a work day.

A *continuous* flow of tasks and activities means that there is always another task, another activity, or another project in a pastor's work queue. There is little to no downtime and few if any lulls in the flow of ministry work. Pastors are on call most days, evenings, and nights for emergencies or other parish needs. The constancy of work can create its own pressures: ministry work can at times seem unrelenting and never ending, yet the perceived importance of pastoral work creates a sense that everything must be done because every work activity or task matters. We heard many stories about days comprising more than twelve hours at work, after which pastors may take work home to continue during what should be their off-work hours.

A *diverse* flow is based on the "switching costs" between tasks. Switching costs are higher when the knowledge, skills, and abilities (KSAs) required to complete one task are very different from those required to complete another. Switching costs are also higher when the modes of thinking and acting differ significantly from one task to another. As an example, consider a pastor who has just finished a meeting to discuss church finances and immediately walks into a meeting to care for parishioners who are facing a major life challenge. Switching costs are costly in terms of cognitive effort, behavioral control, and emotion regulation. It takes a lot of mental, physical, and perhaps even spiritual energy. When experienced over longer periods of time, work of this kind can be stressful and exhausting. It can severely diminish a pastor's resilience. This is one of several important reasons that pastors need regular time off from work, a subject I discuss further shortly.

Multitasking is not a solution. In fact, not only have researchers debunked multitasking as a myth, but research also shows it can be detrimental to our performance and wellbeing (Kraut et al. 1998; Ophir, Nass, and Wagner 2009). Rather than actually doing several things at once, multitasking is really giving short bursts of attention to first one activity and then another. This rapid back and forth of attention undermines performance. Studies also show that multitaskers may be more prone to attention deficit disorder and other learning and performance problems.

(3) Ministry Work Is Punctuated by Unexpected Events

Pastors know and expect that the flow of ministry work can, and likely will, be suddenly and sometimes dramatically changed by problems or issues that upset the tenuous "balance" in work tasks that a pastor has established. I used the term "punctuated" to capture the fact that emergencies are also surprises. As one pastor put it, "The needs of my congregation do not happen within a typical nine-to-five work day. You just never know when or where someone will get sick, injured, or die. Sometimes it can be very hard to feel adequately prepared for emergencies when they happen." Punctuations can also include emails that are framed as requiring immediate attention, the problems or "fires" that arise and must be resolved, or the sudden changes to schedule or deadlines that may occur. These punctuations must be attended to, followed by a rapid return to the queue of normal ministry activities. Pastors must respond to these abrupt interruptions, but figuring out how to prepare is difficult.

(4) There Is Little Structure or Guidance for Prioritizing Ministry Work

Pastors are responsible for prioritizing their work, yet as I have already described, they may have limited control over a significant portion of their work. In addition, deadlines are tight—as soon as one Sunday is over, pastors must begin planning for the next one. Parishioners want their emails or calls answered quickly. Mistakes in prioritizing can lead to misallocation of personal and other ministry resources and may leave important things undone or done poorly. In addition, pastors may feel overmanaged by lay and denominational leaders. Sometimes they feel punished for failing to meet another person's deadlines and priorities. As a consequence, most or all activities and tasks are treated as high priority, and therefore pastors may feel compelled to make time for everything. Consequently, work may never end. One senior pastor described "wading through the daily onslaught of emails" while also trying to fit in daily ministry activities as a "never-ending battle to get it all done."

(5) The Downside of the Turn toward More Digital and Less In-Person Communication

Longer-tenured pastors described a past in which relational connections with parishioners predominated. In the current environment, most communication is indirect through emails, texts, and social media. One pastor told us, "[In the past] the congregation and I knew each other. We talked to each other. We didn't just hammer out a fast email; we took time to share and explain things. That gave us room to really understand and to really connect. Now, a text or brief email is much more common. It is hard to really connect with someone in this way." Whether this remembered style of ministry was ever a reality, the point these pastors are making is that interaction norms in the current ministry environment may be tending toward more arm's-length connections rather than in-person modes of interacting because of increased use of technology. Cell phones, computers, email, and social media can be a boon to pastoral work and pastoral wellbeing. As is always the case with new technologies, it is hard to find an optimal balance, one that capitalizes on the good and minimizes the bad. In this section, I highlight several potentially pernicious outcomes of digital communication.

First, it can truncate communication to just the basic content that a person wants to provide. There is less opportunity for personal connection and for the exchange of care and compassion. Communication is only about "the facts," and so the personal and the person are left out. This can be problematic even in business contexts, in which "facts" are a prime concern. It can be even more problematic in ministry contexts, in which personal connections are a prime concern.

Second, misunderstandings of meanings and intentions may be more likely with these modes because people do not have the nonverbal signals that can be very important for effective communication. Nor do they have opportunities to work out misunderstandings together. A basic feature of human experience is that we are highly sensitive to the negative, especially in interpersonal relationships. We therefore tend to watch for, notice, and dwell on the negative rather than the positive. Furthermore, when communication is incomplete, we tend to fill in the gaps, assuming the negative rather than the positive. For social interactions to be perceived and remembered as positive, there must be a clear and strong positive element that outweighs any negative aspects.

Third, some researchers have argued that these modes of communication can make people feel they are being treated as objects rather than people.

This occurs in part because richer personal connections are difficult to make and miscommunication is more likely, but also because the very mode—email, reports, memos—signals that the receiver of the communication is just another object in the environment rather than a human being with innate dignity (Miller 2017; Ophir, Nass, and Wagner 2009).

(6) External Change Is Rapid

External changes comprise the fast-paced and seemingly constant evolutions and revolutions of the social, legal, and financial contexts in which ministry work is embedded. These external changes can create ministry opportunities, but they can have a direct and negative impact on ministry work and pastoral wellbeing. These external changes can endanger the dignity, safety, health and psychosocial and spiritual wellbeing of both those people pastors are caring for and pastors themselves. In addition, external changes can dramatically impact, for example, the flow of ministry work, the outcomes toward which ministry work is directed, and the way pastors' time and effort must be allocated. These changes may be experienced as requiring that effort be redirected from the ultimate concerns of ministry to concerns of much less importance. For example, one pastor described a months-long conflict with several parents about whether Sunday morning services could be adjusted to make room for playoff games in a youth soccer league. The pastor described many hours spent in meetings and on phone calls and emails over this issue that, as she put it, would have been much better spent doing real ministry work.

THE HIDDEN COSTS OF MINISTRY WORK

John's story is an all-too-common example of the hidden costs of ministry work. As John tried to fit his leadership style into a place where it didn't fit, he ran up against multiple problems. When John described finally "hitting the wall," it was after years of trying to carry out a workload that was burdensome. Like many pastors, he was able to deal with it well for quite a long time. What he did not notice was how the burdens of that workload were starting to accumulate. Bit by bit, he was feeling more stress at work and less joy in ministry. These shifts were subtle and therefore easy to overlook or explain away. Because each church member saw only a portion of John's work, they did not have a full picture of everything he was doing. When John asked for time off, several lay leaders questioned his capacity to fulfill his pastoral duties. So John redoubled his work effort, almost literally, by getting up even earlier so he could find more hours for ministry work. Looking back on what happened, he couldn't believe everything he was trying to do. But those small increases in work happened too slowly to notice. And as I have mentioned, no church member took time to understand all that John was trying to do, so the secret hidden in plain sight was that John was struggling to keep up with the demands of his pastoral role. John's condition—overworked, exhausted, and struggling to keep going—was the prelude to burnout. But John did not realize his wellbeing was in such a precarious place. He thought he could keep going, so when he finally fell into full-scale burnout, it was such a surprise that he felt like he was hitting a wall. Most people who reach the deep burnout that John experienced need an extended leave from their work. And a significant portion are not able to return to work. The damage from burnout can be extensive and enduring.

We have conducted interviews with about one hundred people who, like John, burned out. Each person had a descriptive phrase like "hitting the wall," "I crashed and burned," or "It was like I fell off a cliff." Each person thought he or she could go on at least a little bit longer: no one realized the severity of his or her burnout. These stories make clear that declines in resilience often go unnoticed. People overlook the chronic fatigue they experience and keep pressing on. The capacity to "keep grinding it out," another phrase many of these people used, is a cultural norm in most caregiving professions, including ministry. "You just keep going, keep serving"; that was the expectation that John and his church operated on. No one in his church stepped in to help. Furthermore, we live in a culture that describes "quitters" as losers and failures. These are powerful forces that make it very difficult for pastors to notice or address their resilience, and as John's story illustrates, the consequences can be severe.

One important place for churches to begin addressing the deep causes of low resilience and eventual burnout is to help create reasonable workloads for their pastors. Take the six criteria and, working with the pastor, begin to break down the pastor's ministry responsibilities and activities. I suggest a simple but potentially very helpful approach. Find a way to alleviate or end at least one-third of the pastor's duties. Try to reduce the pastor's workload by one-third. For a while, the pastor will feel like he or she is underperforming because his or her days are not overwhelming. But that is the way work should be: most days should end with the pastor feeling energetic, like he or she could give more effort to ministry. Most days should end well, not end with exhaustion.

Chapter Three

Authenticity

This is a reflection from a member of the Flourishing in Ministry team, Kim Bloom, who gathered many of the qualitative interviews:

I met Carolyn mid-morning at her church. She was part of a group of pastors who had agreed to participate in the research study. She was serving as an associate pastor for a medium-sized church in a college town. I knew the senior pastor and he had spoken glowingly of his ministry partner. We met in the new part of the church that included a beautiful larger sanctuary, fellowship hall, and classroom space.

When you meet Carolyn, you can tell immediately that she brings positive energy to her work. She's warm, looks people in the eyes, and speaks openly and easily about her ministry experiences. She's also physically fit and has a relaxed professionalism that conveys confidence. As with every interview, the first few minutes were spent getting comfortable with one another. I learned that Carolyn is married and has two young children. She's not originally from the area but feels at home in the community. The first question I usually ask is about how people entered ministry—the events, the people, the feelings. Carolyn said, "I grew up with a really clear sense of vocation. My mother is a church worker; my grandfather is a pastor. My father is a scientist, with a theological wonder at the universe and a belief of doing what you were equipped for in ways that God can use your gifts in the world. I knew whatever I did was going to be for the good of the world because of God's love." After a period of wrestling with what seemed to be God's call on her life to ministry, wondering if she was drawn to ministry because so many in her family had worked in the church, she said, "As it turns out, I was shaped to be a church person. I'm not sure I could be anybody else if I tried."

Carolyn's first call after seminary was as a solo pastor of a small rural church. She loves the team aspect of ministry and preferred not to have a solo pastoral appointment. But having that opportunity led to positive self- and professional growth, and for that she is grateful. She was called to her current position as an intern to an older and longstanding male senior pastor. He had a top-down leadership style and made all of the ministry decisions. Carolyn described patronizing interactions with him that seemed to question her abilities to be a woman, have a family, and be a pastor. Their understanding and styles of ministry were as different as the generations into which they were each born. She was aware of this difference in every aspect of ministry, from worship leadership to pastoral care to church administration.

Following a capital campaign to build a new addition, church membership languished and the senior pastor retired. Carolyn went from being the intern with this longstanding congregation, a foot soldier to a "Herr Pastor," to being the pastor-in-charge while the church began a search for a new senior pastor.

Carolyn was the first female pastor at this church. While she was secure in her pastoral identity as a part-time intern pastor, she now had a new role that required more pastoral authority. Following a hierarchical male pastor, she was thrust into a role she had not anticipated and provided an opportunity to either develop new skills and capabilities or withdraw from lack of confidence, allowing others to question her authority. It was a year of growth for both Carolyn and the congregation. She describes them as "more or less welcoming" and says that, by the time they called the new senior pastor, older women in the congregation were asking if any female candidates had been considered. Carolyn believed that to be a sign of progress.

She's honest about the challenges and rewards of personal and professional growth during that time. When I spoke with her, she was five years removed from that initial role shift. Reflecting on what she learned about herself, she said, "The last four to five years have been about confidence in leadership." She describes herself as tremendously shy and prefers to sit in the back of the room. But she has learned that she "plays a mean second fiddle" and knows that she can function with authority and grace. Carolyn reflected that often growth comes later than she would prefer, but trying to force it hasn't always lead to positive growth.

Carolyn is a good example of someone who has high levels of authenticity, the third dimension of wellbeing (Kernis 2005; Kernis and Goldman 2006). Authentic people are comfortable in their own skin. They are confident but not cocky, self-assured but not arrogant. Authentic people are honest with and about themselves. They acknowledge their strengths *and* their weakness. An authentic person embraces what they can do well, they feel confident in doing those things, and they also acknowledge the skills, abilities, and knowledge they lack. Authentic people recognize the better angles of their nature and admit to their darker, shadow sides. Authentic people do not foist themselves on the world. Authenticity does not mean saying or doing whatever they want whenever they want, but rather it means being able to act and behave in ways that are more consistent with their true selves. And perhaps most importantly, authentic people have a quiet ego. They are not self-preoccupied nor are they self-abasing. They are self-transcending in that they recognize the value of others and the value of themselves. Authentic people honor both the needs of others and their own needs, but they think much more about other people than themselves. In this section I describe the two foundational elements that create authenticity: self-integrity, which is how we think of ourselves, and dignity, which is how other people think about and treat us.

SELF-INTEGRITY

Authenticity arises in part from how we view ourselves; what social scientists call self-integrity (Cohen and Sherman 2014). There is strong consensus among social scientists that people have a fundamental need to see themselves as decent, moral people who have intrinsic worth and value, are capable and efficacious, and are striving to live a worthy life. Another way of describing self-integrity is experiencing balanced but secure self-worth. *Balanced* self-worth is grounded in *true* self-knowledge: knowing our strengths and weaknesses, our good sides and bad sides, our more noble characteristics and flawed ones. Gaining true self-knowledge, therefore, requires seeking accurate information and honest feedback about who we are and how we show up in the world. Narcissists, for example, have high self-worth, but they fail to acknowledge their negative sides, and therefore their sense of self is grandiose, exaggerated, and unbalanced. Having balanced self-worth means embracing that we are both "fearfully and wonderfully made."

Secure self-worth means that your sense of worth does not vary too much from situation to situation (Crocker and Wolfe 2001; Jordan et al. 2003). A person with secure self-worth recognizes that he or she has room for improvement, but he or she also believes he or she is a person of value. It is not the same as high self-worth, but it is a sense of positive self-worth that endures. Having secure self-worth does not mean we think better of ourselves but rather that we think well of ourselves. Fragile self-worth, contingent as it is on approval of others or on personal achievements, waxes and wanes. Researchers have found that seeking to boost our self-esteem can actually undermine it because we create a thin veneer of high, fragile self-worth rather than a deeper core of balanced, secure self-worth (Jordan et al. 2003). In fact, comparing ourselves to others is one of the surest ways to undermine self-integrity (Fiske 2011; Gerber, Wheeler, and Suls 2018). People with high but fragile self-esteem are much more likely to engage in social comparisons and also to be harshly judgmental of others. Research shows that people with balanced, secure self-worth tend be more accepting of others and have far fewer prejudices.

In Carolyn's situation she might have struggled with low self-worth when people in the congregation preferred a male pastor or questioned her authority as a young female pastor. Fortunately, she had people around her who confirmed her value as a woman, pastor, leader, and human being. Her husband and family have always loved her unconditionally. There were several members of her first church who consistently affirmed her as a pastor. Carolyn said, "After a year as interim, I think they trusted me to some extent," and that early encouragement helped Carolyn feel a sense of dignity as her pastoral identity began to develop. Even so, she has had very difficult experiences: "Then, when I was the pastor, congregants would want a male to officiate when their children got married. . . . I'm sorry if you don't want a woman to marry you; you're going to have to find someone else. In those moments, it was sometimes hard to feel like a pastor." Over time, her sense of self-integrity has grown and strengthened. She describes how the mentoring and friendship of a senior male pastor has been invaluable. His enduring support and encouragement have helped lift her during challenging times. His confidence in her helped to bridge times that she temporarily lacked it in herself. The importance of these relationships in Carolyn's life points to the second part of authenticity: experiences of dignity.

DIGNITY

Dignity arises when we feel that other people respect us. We experience dignity when we feel other people honor our innate value and worth. We experience dignity when we believe that people recognize and appreciate our talents, abilities, capacities, and uniqueness. Dignity, therefore, is a product of our interpersonal relationships, especially our relationships with the people and groups who are most important in our lives: family, friendship circles, coworkers and colleagues, and the people we serve.

Rejection, incivility, and other forms of social mistreatment challenge and impugn our dignity. Research by Kipling Williams (2007; Williams and Nida 2011), among others, shows that "ostracism plunges individuals into . . . a state of abject misery, sending signals of pain, increasing stress, threatening fundamental needs, and causing sadness and anger." Being socially rejected or isolated exerts the same damage to our health as heavy smoking. Even low-intensity acts like being intentionally ignored, receiving unkind looks or gestures from others, or verbal snipes can undermine dignity, especially when these acts continue over time or if they are perpetrated by several individuals. While most people recover from mistreatment in one-time interactions (for example, if a store clerk is rude or another driver shouts something unkind), our sense of dignity is strongly affected by the people with whom we interact the most and those who occupy important places in our social worlds. Even repeated neutral treatment can be corrosive of dignity if it is perpetrated by people from whom we properly expect to receive positive treatment.

The experiences of Dominique, a pastor in a Mainline denomination, illustrates the heavy cost of insufficient experiences of dignity. She is serving in a large congregation with team-based ministry leadership. Her role is heavy on pastoral care, and she is also responsible for maintaining the church website. She is an African American woman in a predominately white congregation. She is single with no children. Dominique is a slight woman, looks younger than her age, and speaks warmly but quietly. In her presence, I felt that she might wish she could be invisible. Sadly, I wondered how many times she had been told, taught, or forced to be invisible.

I asked Dominique how she knows when she is flourishing. She said, "I know work is going well when I can go home from a twelve-hour day and be exhausted and yet be ready to go back to work." Those twelve-hour days often include home and hospital visits to parishioners, but Dominique says, "When you make it across the threshold of their home, into the hospital at the death bed, or the sick bed, those are really the relationships, the connections that are most important." Even on a long and full day of caring for others, she says, "That's where I really flourish, when I know that they are willing to call on me and say, I want you to pray with me, teach me something, love me as I am. Being accepted into those intimate moments, into people's lives is where I flourish."

Dominique clearly has a heart for ministry, for connecting with people at the human level. It's not surprising that when asked about the opposite of flourishing, when she is languishing, she describes the deep pain of being forgotten. "The church knows that I'm single. When I'm not feeling well, for you not to offer me a bowl of chicken noodle soup, I don't like that, I feel forgotten, I feel unimportant, and that hurts." Unfortunately, Dominique's story is not unique, and it illustrates how even neglectful but not openly disrespectful treatment can be painful. Many pastors described similar experiences: "Some church members seem annoyed with me when I'm sick or when I feel tired. I guess I am just not supposed to have needs."

There are disturbing stories from many pastors who describe being belittled, marginalized, and disrespected by congregation members. Women tell stories of inappropriate comments about clothing and appearance, being forced to receive unwanted hugs and kisses. Many pastors have felt ignored during times of personal crisis, as if the pastor doesn't experience pain and suffering. Single clergy experience higher expectations to cover holidays and long hours because they don't have a spouse or family. These are some of the many ways that pastors feel a lack of dignity. And most disturbing, we heard stories of how churches do not respect pastors with sufficient pay and resources. Dominique said, "I was making too much to qualify for food stamps, but wasn't making enough to afford food for the month, and the church was doing nothing to help with that." Research clearly shows that these pastors will experience a diminished sense of dignity over time. This, in turn, will negatively impact the pastor's wellbeing. It is the rare person who can withstand chronic exposure to even relatively low-intensity incivility and not be affected negatively.

The "sticks and stones" myth implies that "strong" people are somehow impervious to mistreatment by others. This is a terrible untruth. In fact, the only people who are not affected by the treatment of others have aberrant pathologies. Sure, we should aspire to be less sensitive to minor social slights, and it would be helpful to have high enough resilience to withstand more significant mistreatments. But everybody is affected by the persons with whom they interact the most. This is a fundamental part of being human. And so pastors' sense of dignity is, naturally and properly, shaped by the way they are treated by family, friends, and church members, among others.

THE BENEFITS OF AUTHENTICITY

An authentic person, then, has a positive, balanced, and secure self-image. This self-image is based on true self-knowledge, a full and accurate understanding of his or her best self and his or her broken, sinful self. An authentic person also experiences dignity from others. When he or she acts in ways that are authentic to his or her true self, he or she experiences honor and respect from others. He or she feels appropriately supported, affirmed, and cared for by the people with whom he or she interacts the most. And as I have noted, scientists regard authenticity as a basic human need: without it, our wellness and our wellbeing will be significantly diminished (Davis and Hicks 2013; Kernis and Goldman 2006).

Authenticity has many other benefits. Authenticity creates intrinsic motivation to grow and become a better person and a better pastor. Authentic pastors are much more likely to learn how to do new things, develop new capabilities, and acquire new knowledge. Because they are more other-oriented than self-oriented, authentic pastors tend to be better leaders, more capable teammates, and more effective agents of positive change. Authentic pastors have fewer incidents of interpersonal conflict and, when they do, they manage conflict better. They are hardy, more resilient, and cope better with even very serious adversity (McAdams 2013). So authenticity is not only good for a pastor's wellbeing; it is also good for the church the pastor serves, the pastor's family, and the pastor's ministry.

I find that authenticity, like happiness, can be a theologically complicated aspect of wellbeing. I have often heard pastors describe their aspirations to diminish themselves in an attempt to "disappear so that God can appear." I understand the desire to be humble and to avoid thoughts and acts that are self-aggrandizing. An exciting new area of research provides interesting insights into how authenticity can create the kind of humility that leads to both effective pastoral leadership and flourishing. Researchers are finding that when authenticity is experienced consistently over time, it leads to a quiet ego (Wayment and Bauer 2008). The term "quiet ego" refers to having an unpretentious sense of self and low self-focus. Some researchers use the term "self-transcending" humility to describe how a quiet ego leads to a focus beyond the self. People with a quiet ego spend most of their time thinking of others and very little time thinking of themselves. Because they experience self-transcending humility, people with a quiet ego have an open, teachable mind-set and have a high willingness to admit mistakes. They report having many more deeply spiritual experiences. And yet they also seem to pay enough attention to themselves to engage in appropriate self-care.

Researchers contrast self-transcending humility with another kind referred to as self-abasing humility. Self-abasing humility arises from having a lowly opinion of oneself; being meek; and having a low estimate of one's importance, worthiness, or merits. Interestingly, studies show that those with self-abasing humility spend a significant amount of time in self-thought as they strive to renounce their selves. They are passive, averse to taking even appropriate risks, and can be paralyzingly meek. They are tenuous and worried in new situations. They tend to resist change, likely because they have little self-confidence in their abilities to adapt and grow. Their meekness can lead them to withdraw from social situations. Because they tend to be uncertain about their own capacities, they often struggle to perform well in the social roles they are expected to fill. Their attempts to deny themselves also seem to cause them to overlook or forgo appropriate self-care. In a strange and sad way, when people try to renounce and abnegate themselves, they almost always think a lot more about themselves, but these are thoughts about their inherent worthlessness and fundamental lack of value. From the perspective of science, this is a futile and detrimental way to think about oneself. Authenticity, and the quiet ego it can foster, may be the better path toward humility.

Carolyn is authentic, but her story makes clear that authenticity is not something that we achieve and then it never changes. Authenticity is a way of being in the world, and it seems to be essential not only for flourishing but also for being effective in pastoral ministry. Carolyn says it would be terrible if some part of her isn't deeply sad and crying because a beloved parishioner is dying, but she isn't going to fall apart. She recognizes that as the pastor her role when her church experiences the death of a beloved member is to be an inviting and comforting presence, whether there's grief or conflict. She said, "I'm not faking it when I say we're going to be all right because my theology says, even if this is hell, we're going to be all right. I may well go home and lose sleep, but I know this to be true." She knows people who are experiencing "dark nights of the soul" and struggling to be authentic in their ministry. She said, "I can't preach out of anything except my own experience of God, and that involves being a falling-apart human being. That's certainly what I find as Gospel, when I hear it from other people, is not to be a preacher that will now give you pure theology from on high or the ten best ways to do X, Y, or Z, but of resurrection."

THE STATE OF AUTHENTICITY AMONG PASTORS

How are pastors doing with their authenticity? As was the case with daily wellbeing and resilience, there are positive trends but also some cause for concern. Almost one-third of all pastors, both men and women, report having very high levels of authenticity. Among this group, their experience of self-integrity and dignity are very strong. Another 50 percent of pastors report moderate levels of authenticity. So while this group is not in the danger zone, there are signs that some of them might be moving downward in their authenticity. The majority of pastors in this moderate-authenticity group also report moderate to low levels of self-integrity. Some of this may be because of a desire to be modest and humble, but even so, these results are cause for concern. These pastors seem to be more aware of their weaknesses and brokenness and less aware of their strengths and most positive characteristics. Of all pastors, only 5 percent report high levels of self-integrity, which suggests that even some of those in the high-authenticity group may be sliding downward as well.

Here theologies play an essential role in how pastors think about themselves. The fear of pride runs high among pastors. But self-integrity is not pride—it is not arrogance, narcissism, or inflated self-esteem. Recall that self-integrity arises from balanced, secure self-worth. How can theologies support pastors in embracing their skills, talents, and gifts? How can theologies help pastors find their way to a quiet ego rather than striving for self-abasement?

The data are very grim for the 20 percent of pastors whose authenticity is severely compromised. Self-integrity and dignity are both very low in this group. These are pastors whose sense of call to ministry is in jeopardy. We do not know how many of these clergy still have the capacity to be effective pastors, but we know it would be improper to assume most of them are unfit for ministry. Many have been among the walking wounded of ministry in that their pastoral identity has been severely diminished. These pastors need support and help to discern whether their calls are still viable. They need help in restoring their self-integrity and support in determining whether ministry or some other vocation is where God is calling them.

THE ROOTS OF SELF-INTEGRITY

I have described self-integrity as arising from a balanced, secure, and positive sense of self. Another term for sense of self is "identity," and in this section I share more about the broader research on identity and also our research specifically on pastoral identities. Our identity is the way we understand who we are, what makes us the unique person God created us to be. So another way of defining self-integrity is having a balanced, secure, and positive identity. Over the past several decades, researchers have conducted hundreds of studies to better understand our identities, how they form and change, and what kinds of identities and identity development leads to positive outcomes (and what kinds create problems for people). We now know, for example, that people who have self-integrity—a balanced, secure, and positive identity—enjoy many benefits. They tend to have higher daily well-being and stronger resilience. They have better interpersonal relationships, including better marriages. They are positive leaders and valued work colleagues. They adjust well to myriad different life changes and challenges. Research shows, for example, that people with self-integrity deal very well with health challenges. They adjust much better and much faster to personal losses, such as the death of a loved one. People with self-integrity continue to grow and develop over their entire lives, especially in their senior years. They are vibrant, alive, and contributing to the lives of others and to the world around them. People who lack self-integrity face myriad problems, from chronic low self-esteem to difficulties dealing with even simple life challenges to limited capacities for growth and positive change.

Having discovered how important self-integrity is, I want to turn our attention to understanding how our identities develop. This has been an exciting area of research, one that my team and I are deeply involved with, and hundreds of studies over the past decade have produced many important insights. Among the most important of these insights is how our identities form and how they are stored in our brains. Our identities form as life stories, and our brains write them into an autobiography of our lives, what researchers call a life narrative.

In many ways, then, we are living storybooks. Everywhere we go, we carry around hundreds, even thousands, of memories about our lives. Our brains store these memories in the form of an autobiography we are creating throughout our lives. This is truly an amazing capacity. Unlike a computer that just records facts and data, we have the capacity to remember much more. We can remember not only the facts of what happened but also how we felt and how others felt about what happened. We can remember what past events and people meant to us, how they impacted our lives, and how some of those people shaped who we are today. And we weave these stories together into a very special kind of memory that researchers call our life narrative. Researchers have found that each of us has this amazing mental story-writing capacity whether or not we *think* we are writers. And whether we realize it or not, we have all been writing our own autobiographical life narrative every day of our lives. One of the pioneering researchers in this field, Dan McAdams (2013), describes a life narrative as

> the internalized and changing story of your life that . . . ties together the many different aspirations you have and roles you play into a meaningful narrative framework. The story spells out how you believe you have developed over time and where you think your life is going. The story suggests what you believe to be true and good, and how you expect to live up (or not) to those standards. The story serves as a flexible guide for the future and an historical archive for making sense of your past. The story is unfinished, complex, contradictory at times, and subject to considerable revision. It may contain many different plots, scenes, characters, and themes. The story situates you in an adult world where other people have their own stories, some of which may be similar to yours. The story is in you, in your mind, even if you rarely focus consciously on it. You carry the story around with you, and you share aspects of it with other people, especially when they share aspects of their stories with you.

Our identity and our life narrative, then, are the same thing: it is the story of who we are, how we came to be that person, and who we think we will be in the future. Hundreds of studies show that McAdams is right. We know we are much more than a list of facts. You can test this yourself. Ask someone about an important time in their past and they might start with a few facts— "I went to Shawnee Mission South High School. I was an okay student but pretty shy"—but quickly they will tell you stories: "I was so uncomfortable at school that I waited for the morning bus a block away from the stop so I wouldn't have to talk to other students. I always sat in the back of classrooms so I could fade into the background. In between classes, I acted like I was getting something from my locker, but I was really just trying to avoid being seen." Those are parts of my high school life narrative. And just like you, I have written many chapters and stories in my life narrative (my chapters get much happier after high school), and I am still writing and rewriting my life narrative each and every day.

This discovery that our identities take the form of life narratives is regarded by researchers as groundbreaking because scientists now believe it is an essential part of human experience. Hundreds of studies have been devoted to studying our life narratives, including many on how our life narratives form. Essentially, we "author" or "write" our life narratives bit by bit, section by section, and chapter by chapter. This process of authoring begins in adolescence and continues throughout our lives. We are writing our narrative identities virtually all of the time as our lives unfold.

One of the most devastating effects of Alzheimer's disease is that people lose themselves. At some point, the person they were seems to have disappeared. Medical science has discovered why. One of the first things this terrible disease does is destroys the story-writing capacity of the brain. This is why one of the first things that happens to people suffering from Alzheimer's disease is that they can no longer remember recent events. Their brain cannot write stories about what just happened. Then the disease destroys parts of the person's brain that store his or her life narrative. It erases the stories of his or her life, a chapter at a time, until that person's memory of other people, of his or her life, and even of him- or herself disappear.

Our life narratives are organized in many ways like the chapters in a book. We have chapters set aside for important life periods like childhood, being a teenager, high school, early adulthood, and so on. We have special sections for the important experiences like going to college, falling in love, getting our first job, and—important for my research—becoming and being a pastor. Our life narratives have a cast of characters. We are, of course, the main character or protagonist in our life narrative, but there certainly are other people, some who play major roles like parents, spouses, mentors, and best friends, some who serve in important supporting roles like certain teachers, coaches, and bosses, and still others who make cameo appearances like the first person we had a crush on or that difficult professor who made seminary a challenging experience. All of the people who show up in our life narratives had an impact on us, for better or for worse. Our narratives tell who they are and why they matter.

It turns out that there are many advantages for our wellbeing of having our identities in the form of life narratives. One advantage is that stories are flexible. They can be told in different ways. Just like an author in the midst of writing a book, we can change our life stories; we can even change chapters about our past. We can, for example, reinterpret an event from our past or change our perspectives on what a particular person meant to us. The past does not have to haunt us because we can rewrite our life stories so that we remember and understand our past in a better light. Another advantage is that we can write chapters about the future. If our identities were only facts, there would be no way for us set goals for our future or to imagine how we might change and grow. Because we are story writers, we can undertake what scientists call "mental time travel," which means we can imagine things we hope (or fear) will happen and then set goals and make plans for that imagined future. We can imagine the kind of person we want to (or fear we will) become and then take purposeful action to grow and become a better person. We also store our hopes, dreams, and plans for the future in these forward-looking chapters, where they can shape the aspirations we strive for, the goals we set and pursue, and the ways we grow and change.

For researchers, studying life narratives is a treasure trove of wonders. But there is much that each of us can learn about our wellbeing generally and authenticity specifically through this lens of identity as a life narrative.

INTEGRATED NARRATIVE IDENTITIES AND WELLBEING

Our research and other studies show that certain characteristics of our narrative identities are major determinants of our wellbeing, especially our self-integrity. I want to take this idea of authenticity a bit deeper now and introduce two characteristics that are fundamental building blocks of self-integrity. One characteristic is complexity. I already alluded to complexity when I described self-integrity as comprising our strengths and weaknesses, our most worthy characteristics and our sinfulness. We can even be confounding and contradictory. Sometimes I am very extroverted; at other times I am a recluse. How can I be both and still feel like the same person? This points to the second characteristic of self-integrity: having a life narrative that integrates all of the many important stories in our lives and all of the complex and contradictory aspects of who we are in such a way that we feel like a whole person.

A bit more about complexity: As I have already noted, each of us has a variety of different traits, dispositions, characteristics, and preferences that make each of us unique. For example, most of the time I am an extrovert. I like being with people and am energized by interacting with others. But each day I also need time alone. If you happen to try to talk to me during one of those times, you might find me to be aloof, even disagreeable. Another example is that I really enjoy coming up with new ideas, and I seem to be good at it. Details and structure can frustrate me—"Let's get out of the weeds," I often say. But there are parts of my life in which I want order and organization. I'm writing this on my computer, and I have meticulously organized thousands of files (at least in a way that I understand). So I am free thinking and detail averse in some ways but also organized and finicky about details in other ways. There are other, more frustrating (at least to other people) ways that I am complex.

We also have a complex set of relationships and social roles that are parts of our identities. I am husband to Kim, father to Nicholas and Keaton, father-in-law to Maíra, professor, Christian, and avid outdoors person. Each of these is a core part of my identity. Many of these parts of my identity are intricately bound with other people and with the roles I fill. When I say "I am Kim's husband," then Kim is deeply connected to that aspect of my identity. When I say "I am a professor," then the larger community of scholars and my sense of membership in that community is connected to that aspect of my identity. If I have a complex identity (and I hope I do), then it comprises these and many other diverse aspects of who I am.

So we are complex, even complicated, and our identities must include all of that wonderful messiness. Sometimes life gets complicated by the ways these different parts of our identities clash. Think of the dual roles that working parents fill—both roles are major life commitments and self-definitional for these adults. But research shows that complexity is not only a reality for most of us, but it is also actually a good thing for many of us. Maintaining work-family balance can be difficult, but having both enriches my life immeasurably. Furthermore, if things are not going well at work— say one of my studies gets rejected for publication by an important academic journal—I still have a wonderful marriage to go home to. I will still be frustrated by my "failure" at work but because of "success" in my role as a husband and father, I can still maintain balanced, secure self-worth.

Unfortunately, my team and I have had the sad experience of interviewing pastors who do not have a complex identity—being a pastor is all they are. Several years ago I interviewed the wife of a long-service pastor who told me that, even when he was alone with her, he was still "Pastor Joe." He treated her, his children, and his grandchildren just like his other parishioners. The most important relationships in his life suffered greatly because of his one-dimensional identity. As a result, he was protective of his pastoral identity and he became inflexible and rigid, unable to change or adapt. He was moved from one church to another, lasting no more than a few years before some problem or conflict arose. We think this may happen more often to men, who invest almost all of themselves in their pastoral role. Marriage, family, and everything else in their lives are sacrificed to their ministry. Science suggests these pastors are in a very precarious situation. If something goes wrong in ministry, then the foundation of their identity is in jeopardy.

An *integrated* life narrative captures all of the many rich and varied characteristics, traits, dispositions, preferences, skills, knowledge, social roles, and relationships that make us who we are, and it brings unity— integrity—to this great variety. Said differently, self-integrity is the result of a complex but integrated life narrative. Research shows that people who have a complex, integrated life narrative—they have self-integrity—are both adaptable and resilient. They can learn, grow, and adapt to change because they have a clear sense of self—they can see what needs to change, they understand why they need to change, and they can see how to change. People with complex, integrated narrative identities are open to constructive feedback and criticism, in part because there are aspects of their identities that are not challenged by feedback. If being a professor dominates my identity, then I will likely perceive any challenge—a complaint by a student, some constructive but still negative feedback from a colleague—as a challenge to the whole me, not just part of me. But when being a professor is one important part of my identity among several others, I still have secure parts of my identity that allow me to be more open to dealing with disappointment at work.

LIFE NARRATIVES, QUIET AND FLOURISHING

Our research clearly shows that a complex, integrated life narrative is essential for flourishing in ministry because it creates the secure foundation for *being* a pastor. I have mentioned several reasons related to increased personal growth, capacity for adaptability and positive change, greater resilience, and deeper meaning in life and in ministry. A complex, integrated narrative identity also enables pastors to be excellent in their ministries. Such pastors have clarity about who they are as a person and clarity around who they are as a pastor. They know what they can do well and feel confident in doing those things. They also know the skills and abilities they lack, so they are willing to rely on others for help. Pastors who know what they really believe in, who have clarity about their core values and beliefs, can find meaning in even the most challenging ministry contexts. And they are able to speak the truth in love, both compassionate and courageous as they strive toward excellence in ministry. Pastors who have a complex, integrated narrative identity are more adaptable because they know how to bring their best selves into new contexts, and with confidence in their strengths and awareness of their weaknesses, they are more open to change. It is from this kind of integrated life narrative that a quiet ego emerges.

I am convinced that pastors who are excellent leaders have a quiet ego (Avolio, Walumbwa, and Weber 2009). This is an area of research that my team and I will explore in the coming years, but it is straightforward to connect the research evidence we have so far about self-integrity, authenticity, and quiet ego to the essentials of great pastoral leadership. In chapter 5 I share what my team and I have learned about how an integrated life narrative and self-integrity form. In addition to providing insights that are helpful for seminaries and other pastor formation efforts, the results of this research also provide insights about how to help even long-tenured pastors strengthen their identities, foster a quiet ego, and grow in their capacity for excellence in pastoral leadership.

Chapter Four

Thriving

Meaning, Purpose, and Connectedness

Thriving has very ancient roots, going back at least to the Greeks in the fourth century BCE and perhaps to Jewish culture even earlier. Aristotle is regarded as the first person to formally study and write about this dimension of wellbeing, so researchers have adopted his term *eudaimonia* as our technical term for this dimension. Unpacking the word *eudaimonia* provides some important insights into thriving. The Greek *daimon* refers our state of being, our soul or spirit, and the prefix *eu* refers to good or well. So more literally translated, *eudaimonia* is having a good indwelling spirit. Philosophers often translate this as living a meaningful and purposeful life. Researchers are still searching for more precise answers to what thriving is, but there is strong consensus that it includes at least three elements: (1) an overarching system of beliefs, values, and virtues that provides structure and guidance to life (meaning system); (2) a sense of contributing toward important life goals that arise from that meaning system (purpose in life); and (3) experiencing strong, positive connections with other people, especially those with whom we share common beliefs and values (positive connections). A deeper look at each of these elements helps us gain a richer understanding of thriving.

MEANING SYSTEM

In the 1950s, Edward R. Murrow hosted a radio show titled *This I Believe* in which he explored "the personal philosophies of thoughtful men and women in all walks of life. . . . [They] talk out loud about the rules they live by, the things they have found to be the basic values in their lives" (*This I Believe*).

Pearl Buck ("My faith in humanity stands firm"), James Michener ("I believe that all men are brothers"), and Jackie Robinson ("I believe in the power of free minds and free hearts at work") are among those who shared their beliefs on the radio. This program was recreated in 2005 on National Public Radio and, once again, famous people shared from their personal philosophies. Novelist John Updike believes "most instinctively . . . in the human value of creative writing"; Colin Powell shared, "I believe in America and I believe in our people"; and Sister Helen Prejean believes in the importance of turning our beliefs into meaningful actions.

The popularity of these radio programs points to an ancient but enduring insight about human nature: all people have an existential need to find answers to questions like "Why am I here?" and "What should I do with my life?" Modern research concurs with this ancient wisdom. Research studies consistently show that a sense of meaning and purpose are fundamental elements of wellbeing. Meaning arises from having core life values and beliefs that give direction to our lives and set ideals for the kind of person we should strive to become. Our meaning system operates like our life GPS: it points us toward what is most significant and consequential in life; provides us with a path we can follow to live a life of value and worth; sets life goals we can use as milestones to keep us on that path; and provides motivation that keeps us moving ever closer toward an ideal, virtuous life.

People vary in terms of the clarity and strength of their meaning systems. Some people know what they believe, why they believe those things, and strive to live those beliefs in their daily lives. Their meaning systems are clear and strong, and therefore they shape how they view themselves, how they interact with other people, and how they live and act within the larger world around them. Other people seem lost in a world of conflicting or poorly defined beliefs, unsure of where they stand on matters of importance. They are adrift in life without a clear sense of direction. They follow one set of values at work, another set of values at church, and still another when they are out with friends. Their life lacks direction and purpose because they do not have a meaning system.

During my early adult years, I had a sense that teaching would be meaningful to me, but I had never taught a day in my life, so I dismissed those thoughts as baseless. After I finished my doctoral degree, I spent several months clarifying my core life beliefs and values. It was an important but difficult process for me. One of the many positive outcomes of that experience was that I finally understood why teaching would be meaningful for me. One of my core life values is to pursue truth and wisdom that will serve the wellbeing of others. I see teaching as a way I can guide other people toward new knowledge and insights that will benefit them. The subjects I select for my teaching are also chosen with this value in mind. For example, I teach classes about innovation, but I always cast the class around social innovation, creating new ideas that will enrich the lives of other people and make the world a better place. Clarifying my core values was and still is an important part of my thriving.

Researchers have consistently found that a strong and clear understanding of what is meaningful and important in life is one of the most powerful predictors of health and longevity, and it is essential for daily wellbeing and happiness (Markman, Proulx, and Lindberg 2013; Ryff and Keyes 1995; Waterman 2015). When we have such a meaning system, we can invest our lives in things that we know are important. A meaning system inspires us to strive to become our best selves, and it helps us through the darkest moments of life. My team and I have found that people who have a strong meaning system, one with clear life values and beliefs, are much more likely to thrive at work. Their work is meaningful because they have chosen work that allows them to express some of their most cherished values and most deeply held beliefs.

A strong and clear meaning system is also essential for authenticity, especially for self-integrity (Baumeister 1991; Harter 2002). The things we believe in and the core values we hold form the basis for our understanding of who we are and what our place in the world is. Our beliefs and values are also the moral lens through which we make judgments about what is good, true, noble, and worthy, including the evaluations we make about our own self-worth. In fact, if our meaning systems are unclear, we will be unable to have self-integrity because we are adrift in moral space, unable to figure out who we are and what we should do with our lives. I am very concerned that, in a world that is increasingly secular, people will increasingly lack clarity about their core values and beliefs. Of course, we want a society that allows us to choose our values and beliefs, but science is clear that to flourish we must make those choices: we must know what we believe.

PURPOSE IN LIFE

Philosophers, theologians, and researchers all believe that, in addition to finding meaning, we also have an innate need to do something with our lives that we think is important and useful (Seligman 2013; Vaillant 2002). We want to lead a good life, and we want to know that our time on earth has mattered in some positive way. We need a purpose (or several purposes) in life. We can think of purpose in life as a set of overarching goals we strive to achieve and toward which we can direct our best selves. Purpose creates the milestones in our meaning GPS, guiding us to make a positive difference in the world and leading us ever closer to reaching our fullest potential. Purpose is meaning in action.

Purpose is particularly important at work. Given the hours most of us spend at our jobs, we need to know we are using that time well. We need to feel that all of our hard work and effort are making a positive difference in the world. Common among the stories we heard from flourishing pastors was that they could describe, with richness and conviction, the meaning and purpose that are at the center of their calls to ministry. They did not rely on platitudes or broad statements like "God has called me to go and make disciples." If making disciples was part of their meaning and purpose in ministry, then they could describe what specifically making disciples means to them, why it matters, and the specific ways their ministry was oriented toward the purpose making disciples. Of course, "making disciples" is just one example of a life and ministry purpose, and a number of pastors did, in fact, have this as their purpose. Pastors shared others: "to help people find and live out the love of Christ," "to help people have a personal relationship with Jesus," and "to help each person discover what God wants them to do with their life, and help them do that." The important point here is that these pastors had a clear sense of purpose in their lives and in their ministry work.

POSITIVE CONNECTIONS TO OTHERS

A final element of thriving is to feel connected to others in enduring bonds of care, respect, and love (Cacioppo and Patrick 2009). We are fundamentally social beings. This is a scientific fact. Scientific research clearly shows that positive relationships with other people are essential for our wellbeing. For example, research shows that isolation from others can be devastating to our physical and mental health, often having an impact greater than heavy smoking. Positive connections have many important characteristics including mutual care and compassion, emotional support, and unconditional acceptance. In a positive relationship, we feel accepted for who we are, supported in the triumphs and sorrows of our lives, and encouraged to grow and develop to our fullest capabilities. When we have positive relationships, we can be our authentic selves, sharing our deepest concerns, fears, and weaknesses and feeling supported and uplifted as we strive to live a life of meaning and purpose. Positive relationships are mutual: we create that space of care, support, respect, and love for those who offer it to us.

We need positive connections in all of the spheres of life, including work. There is often a sense that "appropriate" relationships at work are all about work and nothing more. Anything "personal" is off-limits at work. Of course there are some aspects of our lives that should not be shared at work, but positive connectedness does not require oversharing. It does require engaging people beyond their work roles. Positive connectedness means we feel respected for who we are and accepted and validated for our strengths and talents, as well as for our idiosyncrasies, uniqueness, and even our oddities. I can be very scatterbrained and often poorly organized. Sometimes I flit from one thing to another. In conversations, I often venture off to explore new ideas. The upside of this is that I am creative and able to see new insights in our research. The downside is that I can derail an important conversation, leaving my teammates uncertain of where I am taking the conversation. Nevertheless, I know my teammates accept and respect me, with all my goodness, weirdness, and annoyances. The care they show me helps me harness my creativity in more focused and positive ways.

Wellbeing at work requires positive relationships. We need people who can help us deal with the ups and downs of work life. We need a boss we can trust, one who cares for us and for the work we do. We need friends and mentors rather than just business associates. We need a caring community of people who will support us in the joys and sorrows of our work and people we can support in their joys and sorrows. But social support is a complex topic. Here I map out some of the basic elements, but I want to provide a richer description so that pastors and leaders of all kinds can have a deeper understanding of this vital area for flourishing. I return to the topic of social support in chapters 7 and 8 because it is among the most important factors for our wellbeing, and this is certainly the case for clergy.

THRIVING AMONG PASTORS

Are pastors thriving these days? This is a dimension of wellbeing on which most pastors are doing relatively well. More than a third report experiencing very high levels of meaning and purpose in life and in ministry. Another 50 percent report high levels of meaning in ministry, so more than three-quarters of all pastors find a great deal of meaning in their ministries. Some of the high-meaning-in-ministry pastors also report somewhat more modest experiences of meaning in life. Our interviews suggest that pastors, like many other help and caregiving professionals, sometimes struggle with finding a way to be excellent in their work and also fully engaged in life outside of work, particularly family life. These pastors may be investing so much in work that they are finding work-life balance more difficult to attain. This is another area in which gathering data from more pastors will help us understand work-life issues, especially among pastors who are still actively engaged in daily parenting or other dependent-care relationships.

A smaller but still significant group—about 15 percent of all pastors— reports very low meaning in life and ministry. Again, these pastors are likely to be the walking wounded I discuss in chapter 1. Certainly some of the pastors in this group would be well served if they could find work in another context. But a percentage this high also indicates that there are pastors who could find a way back to effective if not vibrant ministry. They need the proper support and opportunities to restore and rejuvenate their calls to ministry. But like many pastors who are languishing, they feel isolated. They may also be reluctant to ask for help out of concerns for how it might affect their future in ministry.

I have referred to identity, especially in the form of authenticity, as the "heart" of wellbeing because it can be thought of as the vital center for our wellbeing, the place from and through which the life blood of flourishing moves. I want to use a related metaphor and describe thriving as the "soul" of wellbeing. Metaphorically, "soul" might be thought of as the center of a person's moral, intellectual, and spiritual life, the place from which the strength of his or her character arises, the vital center of what animates and gives direction to his or her life. The "heart and soul" of flourishing, then, is authenticity and thriving. When we describe someone as giving his or her "heart and soul," we mean he or she has been able to give his or her very best. This metaphor is apt for describing how authenticity and thriving are the heart of flourishing and ministry excellence. Together, they shape how pastors experience daily life and are the wellspring of resilience. Authenticity and thriving must be nurtured. Untended, they decline almost imperceptibly. In the last chapter, I share ideas from research on how clergy, local churches, and denominations can help pastors develop and sustain these essential dimensions of flourishing.

WORK-LIFE . . . BALANCE?

There are several places in this book that work-family issues would be appropriate, but I have saved this important topic for now because we have a fuller picture of wellbeing and the state of clergy wellbeing, in general, across the four dimensions. Work-family issues cut across wellbeing dimensions. Our data suggest that work-family challenges are experienced by many pastors, especially those who have children in their homes or those who have significant elder-care responsibilities. There is a great deal of research on work-family issues across work organizations, and three major conclusions have emerged (Williams, Berdahl, and Vandello 2016). The first is that work-family challenges are a major source of stress and a major detriment to wellbeing for most workers and professionals. Most working adults in the United States face significant problems in achieving a good work-family balance. The second is that very few organizations are addressing these issues. Third, workers cannot solve work-family problems on their own; they need the help of their work organizations. So there is a pervasive problem that is not being addressed, and worker wellbeing is being undermined by the problem.

Our research shows that work-family imbalance is pervasive for clergy, as well, and they are often left on their own to figure out how to navigate the challenges it presents. One reason is that pastors do find their work deeply meaningful, and they are very devoted to their ministries. They want to be excellent in their work because "I am working for God," as one pastor described it. "God should get my best, and that means my ministry work deserves to get the very best I can give." As I have described, pastors do flourish when they are performing well in their ministry role.

But pastors often face a "flexibility paradox," in that congregants assume that pastors can easily adjust their work so that they can properly attend to their families and meet their work obligations. But as I describe in chapter 2, few if any congregants have an accurate picture of the pastor's ministry responsibilities. They are often unaware that pastors are working a full day on Sunday and full workdays four or five days during the week. The paradox is that congregants also assume the pastor is available for activities or duties outside of normal work hours. As a result, pastors often do not have the flexibility they are assumed to possess. This seems especially prevalent in solo-pastor contexts. As I discuss in the final chapter, creating a shared understanding between pastor and congregation of the pastor's workload and work schedule may help surface this paradox.

Male and female clergy face different challenges. To be sure, some of the challenges in ministry are not gender dependent, but our research brought to light significant differences. For many years, cultural expectations for men have been that work is the central focus in their lives. These cultural norms are particularly strong in salaried jobs, where the traditional forty-hour work week is not enforced by a time clock. The average work week for men has been increasing, with most professionals reporting more than fifty hours as the norm. Male pastors have described feeling similar expectations: their wives would take care of the family, so they should take care of the church. The experience of male pastors is that they must be intensely devoted to their ministries. One long-service male pastor described an experience with his first church. One sunny Friday he had no meetings, so he decided to go home and play with his young daughters. While they were in the front yard of the house, a congregant drove by in his car. He backed his car up, rolled down the window, and said, "Why aren't you at the church? Don't you have important ministry work to do?" Stories of this kind are common, even among younger male pastors.

Returning to John's story, remember that much of his formation reinforced the need to be masculine and that his career was central to who he was as a person. Being fully devoted to work was ingrained in him through his family and his military experiences. When he became a pastor, John expected that he could pour himself into his ministry work and still be able to fulfill his family role well. But as John describes, he had this image that a man worked hard. He had friends who worked in other professions who worked hard, too, and there seemed to be an expectation that, "the busier you were, the better you were at your work," as John described it. "I felt like, if I wasn't working sixty hours a week, I was a slacker." His congregation seemed delighted that he was working hard and "rewarded" John by asking him to do more. John admits that, for a while, he felt good about this: "I thought I was really achieving good results, and I was glad the congregation thought I could do more." But over time, that workload began to wear on John and his family. He described tensions that emerged in his marriage. At that time his wife was, and still is, "one of my biggest supporters. But she needed me, and my kids needed me, but I was always at the church. Even when I was home, I was at the church, thinking about what I needed to do."

John's experiences seem all too typical for males in many workplaces, including male pastors. Looking back, he can see the foolhardiness of this perspective. The point is not that John should have been formed differently; he simply needed to be aware of this formation as he transitioned from an environment that rewarded this part of him to one in which engaging less authoritatively and directionally would serve him well. It took a while for John to hear what people were saying about this and then to know what to do about it. He had candid conversations with the lay leaders of his church about ministry expectations. These were hard conversations because some leaders did not accept that John had to shift his work down so that he could spend more time at home. Now John feels much better equipped to maintain a better work-life balance, but "it is always a work in progress," he noted. He is learning to take advantage of less busy times at work by spending more time with his family. He schedules vacation time and then always takes it. "That is a major change." And he has a small group of lay leaders who are a circle of support for him in many ways, one of which is to help him with work-life issues. "They really support me in taking time off, and they will tell me when I have gone too long without a day away or without a real vacation. And they help me figure things out when ministry work is too much." This circle of support also "stand[s] up for me with the rest of the congregation. They are outspoken: 'Don't ask that of Pastor John; his schedule is already full,' things like that. They really go to bat for me. I can depend on them to help me adjust my own expectations and the expectations of the church."

Women in many work contexts, including ministry, face a different set of challenges. Carolyn's story illustrates these challenges, especially the expectations faced by women in ministry to be all things at work and at home. Many female clergy are in dual-career families, so they face similar decisions negotiating two work schedules, caring for children, and managing home responsibilities. Like many women in ministry, she faced competing expectations from her church, from the larger culture, and even from herself: she had to be a great pastor *and* a great mother. She had to be fully engaged at work *and* still able to "prepare a delicious dinner, help the kids with their homework, and make home a nice place for the rest of the family."

Carolyn was regularly asked by her senior pastor, "How are you managing with your children?" In staff meetings he would single her out specifically, inquiring about whether she was getting along okay. She learned to respond sincerely yet to offer a response that suggested she was getting along as well as he had when he was leading a church and had small children. She noticed that the senior pastor never spoke about any work-family issues of his own, but his children were grown and on their own.

This "concern" was often voiced by parishioners, too. They seemed delighted that Carolyn had young children, commenting on the "energy" the children brought to the church. But when she limited weeknight meetings or worked from home in the afternoons, people in the congregation were less than generous in their thoughts about her ability to work and have a family. Members complained that she was unable to attend evening church activities. She would hear snide comments like "Pastor Joe was able to manage ministry and family without needing all this time off." Like many women in professional roles, including ministry, Carolyn was not willing to confront the possibility that she might have been in any way ill treated or a victim of discrimination. She was determined to figure out how to be a better pastor, a better mother, and a better spouse.

When there was a senior pastor change and the church called a male pastor with young children, the congregation was thrilled. Upon his arrival, the congregation became much more supportive of work-family balance for the senior pastor, and Carolyn of course benefited as well. Her new colleague created space to have safe conversations about their ministries, their lives as pastors, and the many joys and sorrows of ministry life. They worked together to create better work-family balance for both of them. For example, they shared their family schedules so one could cover ministry duties when the other needed or wanted to be at home. They created a team of lay ministers who were trained to provide pastoral care, and the pastors and this team rotated through staffing the "care line," a phone that members in need could call. One of the two pastors was available for emergencies, but the lay team was proficient in dealing with all but the direst situations. The two pastors forged a healthy working relationship in which the congregation was able to celebrate their ministries and families.

It is important to note that it took a male pastor to help the congregation realize that a pastor needs to flourish at both work and home. Carolyn is very clear that this new senior pastor created opportunities for her that she would not have been able to create on her own.

In many ways, churches and denominations are promulgating a work culture that pits two fundamentally important social institutions—ministry work and family—against each other in ways that can place great strain on their pastors and their families. This culture is at odds with the ideal of a caring, loving community that supports families and individuals. This is, of course, an unintended situation, but it does parallel the culture of society at large. Leading the change to create truly nurturing work-family dynamics would be a remarkable gift to pastors and church members, and would create a compelling example for other work organizations.

Chapter Five

Pathways to Ministry

We now have a framework for understanding flourishing: it is high levels of daily wellbeing, resilience, authenticity, and thriving. We have found consistent evidence in our research that there are trajectories of wellbeing, which refers to the fact that some pastors seem to flourish over long periods of time. Even though they go through low points or struggle with wellbeing for a time, they seem to return to flourishing. Other pastors seem to struggle throughout their time in ministry, never quite able to experience and sustain high wellbeing across all four dimensions. It is as if pastors get on a trajectory of flourishing or a trajectory of languishing and ill-being. I am simplifying these complex patterns, and there are certainly some pastors who do not fit neatly into either trajectory, but in general we can place pastors in one of these two trajectories. Our data also suggest that pastors get into one or the other of these trajectories early in their ministry lives. Within the first five to seven years, a pastor is likely to be in either the flourishing trajectory or the languishing trajectory. What determines which of these trajectories a pastor falls into is whether a pastor develops and sustains an authentic pastoral identity and is thriving. If our insight is correct—and I think it is—then developing authenticity and thriving early in ministry is essential for long-term flourishing.

This chapter and the next focus on what we have learned about how the heart and soul of a flourishing, authentic, and thriving pastor form; what kinds of formation lead to and support flourishing; and what is required to sustain authenticity and thriving.

BECOMING A PASTOR

When I first began to research this topic, Eugene Peterson's (2011) memoir of becoming and being a pastor had just been published. I have returned to this memoir many times because it captures in rich and wonderful ways what we have found in our research.

Eugene Peterson (2011) describes how his identity as a pastor "coalesced" slowly through "seemingly unconnected, haphazard events and people" who "turned out to be organic to who I am." He describes how his pastoral identity did not form through a well-ordered process nor in a thunderous moment nor by mimicking another pastor's experiences. It was a "haphazard" process, as he describes it. Peterson describes his experience this way: "William Faulkner was once asked how he went about writing a book. His answer: 'It's like building a chicken coop in a high wind. You grab any board or shingle flying by or loose on the ground and nail it down fast.' Like becoming a pastor." He had to find his own way, and he was blessed with a loving spouse and wise guides who helped him along the way. Importantly, he describes that his pastoral identity was a blend of taking on the dispositions, responsibilities, and ways of being required to be a pastor but in ways that fit his true self. He writes, "It was a good feeling, this vocational clarity, a way of work that fit who I was. Not just a job so that I could make a living, but a way of living that was congruent with what I had spent all my life becoming." That is authenticity. And that is how an authentic pastoral identity forms.

Lillian Daniel (Daniel and Copenhaver 2009) also describes a journey into an authentic pastoral identity, one that began with playing in punk rock band. She played bass, and the band was good enough to tour. It was a life she loved, but she had felt that Divine nudge, and so she "broke up the band" and followed her call to the ministry. Daniel writes honestly about these beginning times. She worried that seminary would change her for what she imagined would be the worst: "I'll never be cool again," she lamented. "And I wasn't." She remembers going to seminary "carrying a boatful of ego, attitude, judgmentalism, and insecurity" and leaving plagued by doubts— "Was I called? Was there a place for me in the church?" "Would anybody ever take me seriously as a minister?" Powerful people openly challenged her call to ministry. A committee of lay leaders at her home church described Daniel as having "no discernible gifts for ordained ministry whatsoever." Like the unexpected events in Peterson's haphazard journey, Daniel describes surprises—"I had always imagined that the first time I tried on the ministerial role I would be in a pulpit, but instead I was in a mental hospital"—that turned out to be an important, formative experience. She describes her journey to become a pastor as a slow process of "realizing" her own authentic pastoral identity, a process she notes did not take place in "a one-

and-only moment. It wasn't that week, or the next week, or even at the moment of my ordination, two years later. It [happened] slowly, in all the weeks over all the years."

In these stories we see two unique journeys of two unique individuals who crafted their own authentic pastoral identities and yet, in very important ways, there are deep similarities between them. Their unique pastoral identities and the authentic ways they have lived into the pastorate are also manifestations of more universal understandings of what it means to be a pastor. As different as they are, I imagine that if these two pastors had a conversation about their ministries and identities, they would find many similarities and parallels. But the stories of these pastors also illustrate that becoming an authentic pastor begins with knowing who one is as a *person*. Being an authentic pastor begins with true self-knowledge of who one is as a person—knowing one's strengths and weaknesses, good sides and bad sides, more noble and more flawed characteristics. When someone tries to be pastor without knowing themselves first, they are, to use a biblical metaphor, building their identity on sand. Becoming a pastor begins with a complex, integrated life narrative, and it is on that rock-firm foundation that an authentic pastoral identity can be formed.

Eugene Peterson (2011) captures another key insight when he "insist[s] that there is no blueprint on file for becoming a pastor. . . . The ways in which the vocation of pastor is conceived, develops, and comes to birth is unique to each pastor." I wholeheartedly agree. Our research confirms Peterson's assertion in many ways. The old adage to "fake it until you make it" is very bad advice for pastoral formation. As one long-service pastor put it, "You try to be something other than what God created you to be, but that will never work. The only person you can be is the one God created you to be." Plain spoken but very wise. To flourish and to be effective in ministry, pastors have to be authentic to themselves.

At the same time, there are common features to the role pastors play in church—preacher, teacher, counselor, caregiver—but there is no one-size-fits-all way of being a pastor. Pastors who flourish are able to craft ways of enacting these common ministry responsibilities that are authentic to their own, unique gifts and graces *and* that create effective pastoral leadership. No flourishing pastor attempted to redefine the role of pastor in his or her own image. They aspired to be a pastor in ways that were consonant with dispositions, habits, knowledge, and ways of being that are essential for any pastoral vocation. So pastors also need to craft an identity that is authentic to the pastorate.

Therein lies both the wonder and challenge of forming an authentic pastoral identity: it is a way of being that fits each individual pastor and also a way of being that is common to all fruitful pastors. Pastors flourish when they are able to craft pastoral identities that are authentic to themselves because they fit their unique gifts and graces *and* are also authentic to the pastorate. Being an authentic pastor means being both unique in some fundamental ways and also similar in some fundamental ways. Forming an authentic pastoral identity is not easy: it takes work and time, as the stories of both Pastor Peterson and Pastor Daniels illustrate.

My team and I have interviewed hundreds of pastors across a variety of different denominations to explore how pastors find and live into a call to ministry. We spoke to pastors in their first few years of ministry to those in their fiftieth. We interviewed first-career pastors and those for whom being a pastor was a second-plus career. We talked to full-time and bivocational women and men and pastors of color; talking to a diverse group of pastors was key to our project. To compare and contrast what we learned from clergy, we also interviewed physicians, teachers, and international aid workers—about two hundred people across these professions—who also experienced a call to their work. We also gathered data on clergy callings in our survey research. Based on all that research, we were able to map the paths (there are three) that clergy followed as they journey into ministry and identify the key milestone experiences that are important for forming an authentic pastoral identity.

In this chapter I share insights from our research into the paths pastors followed as they journeyed into ministry. What this research reveals is the process through which pastors are able to craft authentic pastoral identities. It also reveals the obstacles and missteps that prevented other pastors from crafting such an identity. I highlight how the kinds of ministry contexts pastors experience during their early years play an important role in whether or not they are able to craft authentic pastoral identities. I will describe how the presence or absence of certain kinds of social support is also important. These are idealized paths, meaning I describe the best routes to ministry. By describing the best pastoral formation paths, we can identify how gaps in formation, obstacles, and challenges may thwart full development of an authentic pastoral identity.

PATHWAYS INTO MINISTRY

We found three different paths that pastors followed as they journeyed into ministry. The first, discernment, was the path followed by many first-career pastors. Discernment unfolded over long periods of time, often years, and followed a process of self-discovery, mentorship, imagining possible futures, and an eventual and often powerful acknowledgment of the pastoral call. Discernment was one path through which pastors can form an authentic pastoral identity. The second path, exploration, was followed by many second-career pastors. Exploration involved a search for meaningful work that often began with a secular job and sometimes followed through a series of secular work roles. It was through trying out different jobs that explorers learned about not only their talents and aptitudes but also their deepest values and beliefs. When successful, exploration eventually culminated in a clear sense of calling and the formation of an authentic pastoral identity. But the exploration path also had more pitfalls and obstacles and therefore was more likely to impede the formation of an authentic pastoral identity.

The third path, the thunderous calling, was followed by a smaller group of pastors, both in their first and second careers. Thunderous callings were unexpected and powerful moments in which individuals experienced what they understood to be a divine revelation. By moment, I mean a very short period of time—usually a sudden, audible voice or a powerfully vivid dream. Those pastors who experienced a thunderous calling and then followed a discernment path were almost universally flourishing. However, pastors who experienced only a thunderous calling often struggled throughout their time in ministry, in large part because they did not form an authentic pastoral identity. I offer some insights into why the thunderous calling alone might create challenges for pastors-in-formation.

Our research shows that pastoral identities tend to form, for better or worse, early in ministry, usually by the time pastors are leading their second or third church. This means that most pastors either form an authentic pastoral identity early in their ministry service or they struggle with a fragmented, ill-formed pastoral identity for the remainder of their time in ministry. I describe the kinds of obstacles and challenges that can derail pastors from forming an authentic pastoral identity. The good news for this second group of pastors is that identities can change and often do. With the right support and good developmental experiences, pastors can reform their identities. The insights we can glean from this research is also helpful for pastors who are facing major life or ministry transitions or pastors who have experienced significant difficulties or challenges in their ministries. There is much that can be done to reinforce, strengthen, and grow a pastoral identity.

Discernment

When discernment went well, it was clearly the path that was most likely to lead to the formation of an authentic, valid pastoral identity. It was also the best path to flourishing in ministry. In this section I describe the ideal discernment journey, highlighting all the essential milestone experiences. Any gaps in a discernment journey or missing milestones are likely to create problems and obstacles for pastoral formation.

Discernment often began early in a pastor's life, sometimes as early as childhood, but for other pastors it began in high school or college. Discernment journeys began with a time of self-discovery, gaining what I referred to in chapter 3 as true self-knowledge, learning about the gifts and graces that make each of us the unique person God has created us to be. We find it is helpful to think about three broad categories of true self-knowledge. *Capabilities* are talents, aptitudes, skills, and abilities. Capabilities are the things we can do well in life, including our capacities for excellence in specific domains, such as a skill with math, an ability to deliver compelling speeches, or a capacity to acquire and use new knowledge. An important part of having true self-knowledge is knowing what capabilities you have and what capabilities you do not have. I have always loved music and have longed to be able to sing well. I just do not have that capability.

Personal characteristics are a broad group that includes a variety of natural traits and dispositions. Our personality traits are important personal characteristics, but any characteristic that is self-defining, that you feel is an essential part of who you are, is part of your true self-knowledge. So gender, ethnicity, race, and other enduring traits are part of true self-knowledge. Again, many of our self-defining personal characteristics we properly regard as positive parts of our true self-knowledge. But most of us have personal characteristics that we regard as personally challenging, while others are part of our dark side or our brokenness.

Core convictions are core life beliefs, enduring personal passions, and deeply held moral values that are central to our lives. These form the meaning system that I described in chapter 4. Our core convictions are the things we believe have ultimate value; they are the things by which we understand what is true, noble, honorable, and good.

True self-knowledge, then, is those capabilities, characteristics, and convictions that are part of a person's true self, what he or she views as his or her core being, and who he or she is at his or her essence. My true self-knowledge is what makes me, me. Yours is what makes you uniquely you. Becoming an authentic pastor began with becoming an authentic person. Knowing about one's true self is a fundamental building block for crafting an authentic identity as a person, and gaining true self-knowledge is a key milestone experience of discernment.

Pastors who followed the discernment path—who I refer to as discerners—had many rich stories, spread out over long stretches of time, about how they gained true self-knowledge. These often included some childhood stories, as illustrated by a pastor who said,

> I may have been the only kid in Sunday School that was really interested in Scripture. Even when I was in first or second grade, I was asking my Sunday School teachers to explain Scripture to me. I must have bugged the heck out of those teachers, but they always seemed patient with me. Ever since then, I have loved studying the Bible and its history.

Other pastors told childhood stories of a love of learning or a passion for taking care of animals or people or realizing that they had a talent for music or learning or gardening. They also told stories of learning that they were introverts. Several described how having attention deficit disorder has been both a blessing and a challenge. Women described learning how to live in a gendered culture. Pastors of color described finding self-worth and dignity even in a culture that ostracized and denigrated them.

As discerners entered their adolescent or young adult years, they became introspective, taking time to step back from the busy flow of life to think about, among other things, what they were learning about themselves; to ponder the meaning of their life; and sometimes, to even "try to solve the world's problems," as one pastor put it. In their introspective times, discerners were self-aware, not self-obsessed. Introspection refers to the intentional time discerners took to reflect on themselves, what was happening in their lives, and where they thought they were going in life. As one pastor put it, "I was learning a lot about who I was and who I was not, and so I spent time trying to imagine where God wanted me to go in my life." Some discerners kept life journals, and this was the way they reflected on themselves and their lives. Others described retreats in which they had opportunities to be guided in self-reflection. Still others spoke about good friends or wise elders with whom they had

> these long, deep conversations, about life and God. There was certainly some navel gazing, but it was great to be able to think out loud about stuff that mattered. At the time I didn't know those conversations were anything more than hanging out with a friend. But now I can see they were really helpful because they helped orient me toward where God was leading me.

A third milestone experience of discernment is finding exemplars. Exemplars are role models, people who seemed "comfortable in their own skin" and who were also doing something meaningful and important in life. Exemplars are living proof that a calling is real and that people can achieve excellence in a calling. What makes exemplars so important is that they helped discerners imagine themselves in specific work roles. There were pastoral exemplars, but often there were also exemplars from professions. Discerners often told stories of considering other career options, and this was almost always a good experience because they felt more confident in their calls: they had considered other jobs and understood why they should not pursue those options. Exemplars were cognitive springboards who allowed discerners to imagine whether they could be a particular kind of professional. Eventually, they found pastoral exemplars who helped them imagine themselves becoming a pastor. A basic structure for how exemplars were helpful was "I know about Exemplar A who is a (pastor). I can see a lot of myself in Exemplar A.

Because I see how Exemplar A is a (pastor), I can now better imagine myself as a (pastor)." Consider this story from a pastor:

> I'm this little girl growing up in the '60s. . . . Church, it was always part of our life, but pursuing [the pastorate] wasn't really encouraged. . . . Pastors are men. I never thought someone like me could be a pastor. . . . When I saw [a female pastor], it was like a bolt: suddenly everything was clear to me. All those inklings? All along, they were my call.

Another pastor told us, "I just began to see that I could be a pastor, like Pastor [Joe], he had this deep love for helping people, for preaching God's truth, for being present to people, just as I did. That helped me connect to my call to ministry, and it was something I could turn back to as a reminder." Here this pastor connected his deep love for helping, preaching, and being present to the similar characteristics he saw in his exemplar, and then he used that as a springboard for envisioning himself as a pastor, a way to more fully connect to his call to ministry.

A rich and varied repertoire of exemplars was especially helpful because such a repertoire helped discerners to imagine themselves following a variety of career paths and then to select the path that felt right. They had considered other viable options and ruled them out. Environments that provide a rich variety of exemplars would be particularly helpful to discerners who may otherwise have limited contact with exemplars. Seminaries that, for example, invited a variety of pastors to share their life stories and their stories of discerning their own call to ministry were especially helpful.

Women clergy and pastors of color were often left without exemplars, as the above quote from the female pastor illustrates. Many of the women we interviewed described a long time in which they felt a call to ministry but ignored it because they had no experience with a female pastor. But their first exposure to a woman in ministry dramatically changed their life courses. They finally understood, as the pastor I quote described, that their feelings were indeed a calling to ministry.

Imagining is the fourth milestone in discernment and a very important one. Here discerners gave deep thought to how their true self-knowledge and the things there were learning from exemplars were pointing them toward their calls to ministry. Most discerners had several pastoral exemplars against whom they could compare themselves. And they spent many thoughtful and thought-filled hours probing whether and why being a pastor was their call. As Lillian Daniel writes, becoming a pastor "takes holy imagination just to remember a call, to imagine one, not in the sense that the call is an illusion created by us, but when we imagine, we see what we do not know; we see the possibilities God has for us." Discerners actively sought holy imagination. They had a lifetime of learning about their true selves, they had reflected on themselves and their lives, and they had learned a lot from exemplars about what it took to fill different work roles. Through imagining, they were bringing all of this together in a way that illuminated their call to ministry. Many discerners described that the way God spoke to them was through the way their lives had unfolded. Through imagining, they could see how their lives had added up to a call to ministry. As one pastor described it, "I was beginning see how all those events and experiences were God's arrow pointing me toward ministry."

Discerners also often recounted turning to wise guides to help them. Wise guides are people who know a discerner very well and who can also provide expert advice, sage counsel, and positive support through their journey of discernment. Wise guides included teachers, coaches, pastors, professors, and other elders who were willing to spend time with the discerner. They were sounding boards and sources of insight. They shared from their own life experiences and listened carefully to the life experiences of the discerner. They affirmed the discerner's gifts and reflected on the places in the world where a person with those gifts might fit. They rarely made pronouncements about what discerners should do, instead spending more time listening to the discerner and then offering thoughts and reflections.

Wise guides were particularly important when discerners imagined their calling. For example, a female pastor described the way a wise guide influenced her journey: "My pastor said, 'What are you going to do after college? . . . Have you thought about going to seminary?' and I said, 'Yes, but guys do that (laughing).' He said, 'No, that's changing. Women are serving as pastors. I could see you doing that.' That was when I really began to believe ministry could be in my future." Wise guides know what it was like to be a pastor, and they also know the discerners they guide well. They speak with the authority of experience and expertise and the beneficence of a caring and trustworthy counselor.

Discerners also had significant others—loving parents and family, good friends, caring church members, kind neighbors—who cared about and helped them. They had what researchers refer to as secure attachment relationships, adults who provide a safe haven for discerners. They are people the discerner could rely on for comfort and safety in the face of threats. And significant others provide a secure base, an enduring source of love, compassion, and care, that instill confidence and strength so discerners could explore themselves and then discover and follow their calling. The safe haven and secure base that significant others provide are especially important for women and persons of color who faced an uncertain and often hostile world. "My parents believed in me even when I started to doubt myself," one female pastor told us. "When people told me I couldn't be a pastor because I was a woman, my parents reassured me. They said those people were wrong; they said they believed my call to ministry was true. It meant a lot then, and it still means a lot."

Over time, through the process of gaining true self-knowledge, introspection, and holy imagination, discerners were able to develop many detailed insights into how their true selves were well suited to becoming a pastor. They had dozens of stories about how their lives unfolded in ways that added up to their calls to ministry. A journey of discernment was never neat and tidy: there were often missteps, sometimes dead ends, and usually stories of doubt. Their life stories were messy, like all real-life stories. They spoke about bad decisions that took them down dead ends. They spoke of wandering around lost or being "completely oblivious to what was happening to me." They had false starts. And they faced challenges, crises, and grief-filled moments. There were sometimes surprising coincidences that later turned out to be pivotal moments.

But bit by bit, life chapter by life chapter, their calls to ministry became clearer as their pastoral identities became stronger. At some point, it all became clear to discerners, and then they knew they had a call to ministry. Most discerners, like Eugene Peterson (2011), described a moment of epiphany: "It seemed to arrive abruptly—there it was: Pastor." And so when that sense of clarity arrived, as Peterson describes it, "all kinds of things, seemingly random experiences and memories, gradually began to take a form that was congruent with who I was becoming, like finding a glove that fit my hand perfectly—a calling, a fusion of all the pieces of my life, a vocation: Pastor." But as Peterson goes on to share, he had to live out that calling that was congruent with the person he had spent his life becoming. That is the subject for the next chapter of this book. We turn our attention now to the second pathway into ministry.

Exploration

The second path into ministry, exploration, is more roundabout, a less direct path to ministry. This more circuitous path does not necessarily mean that a call to ministry was any less genuine or that explorers are never able to form an authentic pastoral identity. But explorers lack some of the important milestone experiences that helped discerners. Nevertheless, many explorers found their calling and were able to form an authentic pastoral identity.

As I did with discernment, I describe a positive exploration path, highlighting the essential milestone experiences. Again here, gaps in those milestone experiences likely created problems and obstacles for pastoral formation. Some explorers did struggle to clarify their calling, and they struggled to form an authentic pastoral identity; I highlight why. I have a special affinity for exploration because this is how I found my calling in life. I remember when I first heard stories from discerners and how I wished my life had unfolded in that more direct way. I was a paramedic, then a consultant, then a financial advisor, before I finally tried academia and eventually found my calling in teaching and research. I became a professor much later in life than most of my colleagues. I joke that I was a late bloomer, and there have been times I wish I had found my calling earlier. I share these experiences with many explorers.

One very important difference is that explorers often lack the kinds of early experiences they need to acquire true self-knowledge. Because of this, it took them much longer to develop that necessary foundation of self-knowledge, and so finding their calls to ministry came later in life. There are a variety of reasons why experiences in gaining true self-knowledge are much scarcer for explorers. Perhaps they grew up in underresourced contexts where they simply did not have the kinds of opportunities that discerners did to explore the world and learn about themselves. Perhaps they did not have enough supportive adults—that teacher who took a special interest in them or the church elder who mentored them. Or perhaps their families moved often, so they were constantly adjusting to new environments. Several explorers were raised in farm communities and were the first members of their families to go to college. As they explained it, their parents—kind and loving as they were—simply did not have the background to help them think about any kind of work beyond farming. This scarcity of true self-knowledge made it more difficult for explorers to find their calling. They had to learn about themselves later in life, which was one reason that many explorers answered their call to ministry much later as well.

The way most explorers finally did find their calling was through experimentation. They tried out different jobs, learning about themselves as they worked but always searching for truly meaningful work. Some explorers were very successful in other kinds of work—everything from teaching to nursing to a job in the corporate world to farming—and those experiences were positive for them in many ways. They gained important knowledge and skills. And it was through these work experiences that they gained true self-knowledge. They learned about their talents and gifts, and they learned what skills and abilities they lacked. They clarified what they believed in, what mattered most to them in life. And so while they were successful in other kinds of work, they began to understand what was missing in those jobs: an opportunity to live out their values and beliefs. It was that understanding that eventually led them to ministry.

Another important difference is that explorers often had to journey on their own for long periods of time. They lacked exemplars and so found it very difficult to imagine themselves as pastors. Many women told us that they had felt a call to ministry for years, but until they saw a female pastor, they continued to seek other ways to express that call—director of Christian education, Sunday School teacher, church volunteer. Explorers also often lacked wise guides to help them, and so they had to figure things out by themselves, which took longer. Explorers often faced institutional challenges. Some were told they did not have the right educational background to get into seminary, and so they had to find another route into ministry. Others experienced resistance from their denomination, in some cases because their work history was misunderstood or because their call story was interpreted as less compelling. Several shared stories of being told "ministry is not just another place to try to find yourself," and so they continued to experiment and explore, searching for their calls.

Those explorers who did find their calls to ministry had to be intrepid. Trying out job after job can be arduous and risky. Leaving a job that pays well is not easy, especially if you have a family to support. But explorers were willing to make these kinds of hard decisions because they felt an urging and insistent nudge that there was something else, something more they were supposed to do with their lives. There were moments of despair and dejection—"Will I ever find my calling?"—they had to persevere, following that still small voice. Over time, that sense of calling became clearer until finally they felt ministry was the right place for them. They made one final leap of faith into ministry. For many this was a very risky leap: there was no turning back to their former jobs. They were "all in" as one explorer put it: "Either I was called to ministry, or I was just plain lost. I had thought and thought and thought, and the only way I was going to know was to try. So I jumped."

This leap of faith into ministry was not the end of the challenges explorers faced. Some attended seminary and continued a full-time job to support themselves and their families. Others found alternative paths into ministry, often through a more compressed credentialing process that, while allowing them to undertake pastoral ministry, often seemed to carry with it a status of being less of a pastor than those who were ordained. Many of those explorers who persevered have fruitful ministries and are fine pastoral leaders. They have an authentic call to ministry and an authentic pastoral identity. But knowing the challenges that these explorers endured and the persistence required for them to finally find their calling leaves me wondering how many explorers are still trying to find their ways to ministry.

Thunderous Calls

A thunderous call comes in a powerful moment—an audible voice, a vivid dream, a compelling sign. Thunderous calls are sometimes unexpected and at other times are powerful confirmations of an intuition that has been growing for some time. This path proved to be difficult for pastors if it was the only path they took. Many pastors who experienced a thunderous call were also discerners, and these pastors usually found their way to fruitful ministry. But pastors who only had a thunderous call sometimes struggled. The story of one such pastor illustrates these struggles. He was a construction worker and was unchurched for most of his life. He married a Christian woman and began to attend church. His life changed. He gave up his "sinful and sin-filled past" and accepted Christ as his Savior. A year or so later, sitting in the pew one Sunday, he heard God's voice calling him to ministry. His wife affirmed this call, as did members of the church he was attending. He answered yes, decided against seminary, and went directly into ministry. At the time I interviewed him, he had been appointed to more than a dozen churches in ten years. At each church, "the congregation was not ready for the truth I preached to them." Conflict ensued. The pastor was moved to a new church. And the cycle repeated. This pastor was sure of his call—he had the thunderous experience as his assurance, and yet the history of his ministry indicates something is amiss.

What might explain the struggles this pastor experienced? He leapt into ministry, bypassing the self-discovery, introspection, and self-reflection that are essential milestones for discerners. He told no stories about gaining true self-knowledge other than recounting his rebellious youth. He had no stories of exemplars or wise guides. He was trying to be a pastor but had not developed a specific identity about the kind of pastor *he* could be. He had adopted one, but this identity was more like a role he was playing in a movie.

The challenge with a thunderous calling is verifying that the source of the call *is* God. Confirmation by others can be important depending on who those others are. We found that, when thunderous calls were confirmed by wise guides—other clergy, religious leaders, learned elders, or others who have had experience shepherding people into ministry—those pastors went on to develop an authentic pastoral identity. At least part of what mattered for these pastors was that they undertook the kinds of identify formation work that we see in discerners. They formed a complex, integrated identity—they knew who they were as a person before they began to understand who they were as a pastor. Wise guides throughout their lives were important because of the essential role they played in helping. When these wise guides were missing, the likelihood of confused or erroneous callings was much higher, in large part because pastors did not develop a complex, integrated identity before trying to answer their thunderous call. In other words, they did not know who they were as a person and so had little foundation for imagining who they could be as a pastor.

I want to emphasize again that some pastors who received thunderous calls did indeed go on to have vibrant and fruitful ministries. What seems to be essential is having enough true self-knowledge to first know who you are as a person, an identity that includes all of the fearful and wonderful parts of yourself. That authentic identity as a person is, it appears, the foundation for holy imagination and for eventually forming an authentic pastoral identity.

SUMMARY

Three paths to ministry reflect a way to discover or find a call to ministry. These "ideal" paths can provide insights that can be helpful in several ways. First, the milestones of discernment can provide a way of supporting individuals who feel a call to ministry. For example, providing these individuals with facilitated opportunities to share their true self-knowledge can help some of these individuals create clearer connections between the vocation of pastor and their capabilities, personal characteristics, and core convictions. For others, it might identify the need for further self-discovery or perhaps even help surface incompatibilities between a pastoral vocation and their personal gifts and talents. Second, the milestones of discernment might also be adapted to help people who are journeying into ministry through exploration, especially the many second-career pastors who are likely taking this path into ministry. Again, opportunities to tell their life stories in more complete ways will help clarify whether they have the gifts and graces required for ministry. Among those who do, exposure to a rich repertoire of exemplars would create opportunities for explorers to more fully imagine the pastors they might become and help strengthen their sense of calling as well. Fostering relationships with wise guides would also be very important. I want to emphasize that assigning wise guides is rarely an effective strategy. Relationships with wise guides form more organically to allow individuals to find the deep similarity needed to create truly beneficial mentoring relationships. The best support would be creating opportunities for newer and more experienced pastors to get to know each other more fully as people.

Discerning or finding a call to ministry is in many ways the beginning of becoming a pastor. That call now has to be lived out, and a fully formed pastoral identity must be developed. Fully answering the call requires, as Eugene Peterson (2011) describes it, finding a "way of work[ing] that fit who I was." That is the stage in which an authentic pastoral identity comes to life, the stage in which those who are called to ministry actually become pastors. In the next chapter, I share what we have learned about how that happens. I turn again to Pastor Peterson and highlight how our research confirms his wisdom.

Chapter Six

Living a Calling
and Becoming a Pastor

Finding and answering a calling are the first steps in the journeys that flourishing pastors take into ministry. The next step is to live out that calling. From this point, discerners and explorers followed a similar path, one that resulted in formation of an authentic pastoral identity. This is the period of *integration*, the time in which individuals found a way of being a pastor that was both an expression of their true self that was personally authentic *and* a way of being a pastor that was an authentic pastoral vocation, what I refer to as professionally legitimate. I know that some pastors and leaders do not like the idea of the pastorate as a profession. My use of that term follows William Sullivan's (2005) definition of a profession as an "occupation based upon formal knowledge and trained skill, organized in a collegial or guild-like way, and carried on in the spirit of service." The profession of being a pastor comprises expectations about the knowledge, skills, abilities, codes of conduct, and ways of being that are regarded as essential for all pastors. Pastors who flourish have formed a pastoral identity that harmonizes personal authenticity and professional legitimacy. They are both uniquely their own kind of pastor and also similar to their sisters and brothers in ministry.

BECOMING AUTHENTIC

I want to return to Eugene Peterson's (2011) description of "vocational clarity" as "a way of work that fit who I was. Not just a job so that I could make a living, but a way of living that was congruent with what I had spent all my life becoming." Our research confirms that Peterson is right. Wayne Oates (1982) also emphasizes that pastoral formation is guided by "[a pastor's] inner sense of identity and integrity or lack of it." Oates also asserts that a pastoral identity begins with the pastor's "'personhood' under God. . . . The Christian pastor . . . is an authentic person under God, not just a walking job description." Again, our research strongly confirms Oates's assertion. Our research is clear that an authentic pastoral identity is part of an authentic identity as a person. As I described in chapter 3, when being a pastor is the totality of a clergy's identity, challenges and difficulties almost always follow. Becoming a pastor, then, is finding a way of being that personifies self-integrity. In their early years in ministry, many pastors find themselves facing strong expectations from members of their churches and their denominations to become the kind of pastor those people want. Peterson sees this as well, emphasizing that "those of us who enter into this way of life, this vocation, this calling, face formidable difficulties both inside and outside congregations—idolatrous expectations from insiders, a consignment to irrelevancy by outsiders." Oates also emphasizes, "The struggles of the spirit occasioned by being a real person in the face of the expectations and demands of a congregation genuinely shake the foundations of all preconceptions [of what being a pastor entails]." These strong expectations—what I refer to as identity demands—can undermine the formation of an authentic pastoral identity. Identity demands are imposed on pastors, most often by members of the churches they serve or by the culture of their denominations. Richard Neuhaus (1992) captures identity demands well in his description of what pastoral life is like for many clergy:

> The minister is expected to be preacher, leader of worship, counselor, teacher, scholar, helper of the needy, social critic, administrator, revivalist, fund-raiser, and a host of other sometimes impossible things. . . . Pastors harassed by these conflicting expectations and claims upon time and ability are tempted to embark upon an open-ended game of tradeoffs. Today I'll be a little of this and a little of that, tomorrow I'll be a little of the other things and something else.

He correctly concludes that trying to meet these identity demands is "a certain formula for confusion and collapse." Pastors who flourish find a way to navigate these identity demands, and they do this by forming a pastoral identity that is authentic.

Pastors crafted identities that are authentic in at least three ways. First, they tailored the way they enacted core elements of their pastoral role, things like preaching, teaching, and caregiving. For example, preaching is a core role feature for pastors. That is, preaching is a ministry activity that almost all local church pastors are expected to undertake. When enacting this core role feature, clergy who formed an authentic pastoral identity described adopting a style of preaching that matched their true self-elements. Consider these three illustrative examples of personalizing preaching: "I'm not an inspirational guy, so I am more teacher in the pulpit than charismatic preacher," "I really love stories and storytelling, so that is always a part of my sermons," and "I don't write out my sermons. I pick a topic and read some Scripture, and then on Sunday I just let the Spirit flow and fire me up. I just let go, and God does the rest." Here each pastor embraces the importance of preaching, but each finds a style that is well suited to his or her capabilities and personal characteristics. Pastors who developed an authentic identity found similarly personalized ways of undertaking other core aspects of ministry work.

Caregiving is another example of a core role feature for most local church pastors. Clergy who formed authentic pastoral identities personalized the way they engaged in this centrally important part of pastoral ministry. One pastor explained how this part of ministry was one that she cherished. She valued visiting shut-ins, spending time in the hospital rooms of her church members, and taking time to call church members who were experiencing special joys or difficult challenges. She also found pastoral counseling of great importance in her ministry, another place where this one-to-one caregiving is important. In contrast, another pastor noted that he struggled with caregiving, not out of a lack of care for his church members, but because he was more reserved and introverted. He found that writing personal notes was an effective way for him to provide care to church members. This approach gave him time to think through what he wanted to communicate, and he found it allowed him to make a more personal connection with church members because they appreciated the time and consideration a handwritten note conveyed. Both pastors cared for their church members but in a way that fit their true selves.

Second, pastors formed authentic pastoral identities by expanding the ways they did ministry, adopting new expressions of ministry that allowed them to integrate more of their true selves in their pastoral identities. For example, a pastor with an undergraduate degree in marine biology described herself as "committed environmentalist." She created an annual sermon series on "caring for God's creation," in which congregants were invited to work in the church's community garden. She has continued to do this sermon series each year, and she has added more environment-oriented ministries that help her church "be more connected to our local community." She describes herself as "a pastor for people and the earth," giving voice to how claiming this helped her experience personal authenticity. Another pastor was a theater major in college and had a passion for performing arts. He found that drama, music, and dance could be powerful ways of communicating the truths that he saw as central to the Christian faith. He integrated short dramatic performances into many Sunday worship services. Church members often acted in these dramatic scenes that were related to the sermon theme, such as a modern version of the Good Samaritan story. Here he personalized his way of preaching, and he also found a way to express himself by creating a new drama ministry program at his church. Not only were these very well received by his congregation, but they also created opportunities for the pastor to engage ministry in a way that "felt more natural to me. I can share more of me and more of the pastor I am through those performances."

By personalizing the way they enacted core features of their pastoral roles, and also by expanding the way they enacted their pastoral roles, flourishing clergy were able to be more authentic as pastors. As Eugene Peterson (2011) emphasizes, "The ways in which the vocation of pastor is conceived, develops, and comes to birth is unique to each pastor." Flourishing pastors achieved this by tailoring their pastoral identity in such a way that it allowed them to more fully express their true selves. Said differently, flourishing pastors personalized their way of being a pastor.

A third and essential way that pastors crafted authenticity was by enacting their core convictions, the beliefs and values that lie at the heart of their Christian faith. I have also heard this referred to as a *personal theology*, which draws attention to a pastor's understanding of what it means to be a Christian and to live a life of Christian faith. In chapter 3 I describe the importance of theological fit for pastoral wellbeing. Theological fit mattered for pastoral formation as well. Pastors who formed an authentic pastoral identity were able to express their personal theologies in their pastoral roles. Early in their ministry lives, flourishing clergy were appointed or called to churches that honored their personal theology. Often there was a strong fit between the pastor's personal theology and the theology of the congregation. But even in cases in which there were theological differences, supportive churches created space for new pastors to express their personal theologies. These pastors spoke of how these supportive environments gave them the opportunity to clarify and deepen their personal theologies. They had opportunities to learn more beneficial ways of expressing their personal theology in their pastoral work. And they learned how to create fruitful ministries when they had theological differences with some members of their church.

Personal theologies are central to any pastor's call to ministry. Pastors are called to live out certain essential beliefs and they are called to be pastors whose ministries reflect those beliefs. Pastors who experienced a strong mismatch between their personal theology and that of their church often struggled to develop an authentic pastoral identity. Most of these pastors tried to adopt, or at least enact, their churches' theologies, but this usually proved difficult. This pastor's description represents what we heard from many other pastors: "I found myself preaching things I just didn't believe, but I preached about those things because it's what that church expected of me. It was a very difficult time because I was trying to do the right thing, but I also did not feel I was being honest. At my next church, I was able to preach what I believed to be true. That's where I found my voice."

While I can describe the three ways that pastors were able to form authentic pastoral identities, this formation did not happen in a step-by-step fashion. Remember Eugene Peterson (2011) describes his experience as similar to "building a chicken coop in a high wind." Again, our research confirms Peterson's wisdom. Pastors were able to craft authentic pastoral identities in the middle of ministry work. Forming an authentic pastoral identity was an on-the-job process. Pastors could not develop their identities in the abstract world of seminary. They had to be out in the real world of ministry work. And importantly, they had to have opportunities to improvise and experiment with the ways they did ministry. They tried, for example, different ways of preaching until they found a style that both felt right for them *and* that created fruitful worship services. This means that pastors need the space and latitude to experiment, improvise, and personalize their expressions of ministry. Clergy who were fortunate enough early in their ministries to be appointed or called to churches that welcomed new pastors recalled the benefits they experienced of being in these supportive, open ministry contexts. These churches were patient as the new pastor learned how to fill the pastoral role and figured out their personal styles of ministry. They offered support and encouragement for the new pastor's unique expressions of ministry and constructive feedback about opportunities for improvement and growth. And all of this was wrapped in a community of caring for the new pastor. These pastors said that they knew that church members had a vested interest in supporting them, their families, and their ministries. As one pastor put it, "I knew they cared about me as a person and also as a pastor. It was both kinds of caring that created such a rich place for me to learn how to be the pastor God created me to be." This points to the importance of having early experiences in supportive local church contexts that allow pastors to learn more about the unique pastor God has created them to be and to develop ways of becoming that pastor, one who has a personally authentic pastoral identity.

We have found, however, that these open and supportive ministry contexts are rare. More common are stories about being appointed or called to churches that placed strong expectations on new clergy to conform to the church's expectations. We heard many stories about pastors who were called or appointed to churches that were dominated by a usually small but vocal group of parishioners who imposed their expectations on the pastor. I refered to these as identity demands. The word "demand" is important—identity demands are foisted on pastors in an effort to compel or coerce the pastor to act in certain ways, to express particular attributes or dispositions, or in other ways to conform to the expectations of others. Identity demands allow little leeway in how a pastor expresses or enacts the pastoral role: "We expect a dynamic sermon every Sunday. You have to inspire us." "You need to be more holy; you seem too common. I can't admire a pastor who is common." "We've never had a pastor who didn't hunt. It's hunting season. When are you going out?" These are explicit identity demands, but even more subtly expressed demands can nevertheless be powerful. Pastors of color who serve in predominantly white denominations and women across denominations often find themselves in contexts with identity demands that subtly but strongly signal that their gender or race is not consistent with who a proper pastor is. Women may hear demands expressed more subtly: "You need to be more commanding," "You need to take charge," or more explicitly, "You are too cute to be a pastor." Pastors of color, likewise, may hear subtle and explicit demands: "You're the first black pastor we've ever had. I can't imagine how this is going to work."

Many early-service pastors try to meet identity demands by striving to adapt their pastoral demeanors, styles of ministry, or in some cases their personalities. In the process, these pastors may forestall developing an authentic pastoral identity. When pastors try to fit into the identity demands imposed by others or when strong social pressures compel pastors to do so, then the most likely outcomes are that these attempts will fail, the pastor's identity formation will be stunted or damaged, and neither the pastor nor the church will flourish. As a consequence, they often move forward in ministry with a fragmented or partially formed pastor identity. Because they rarely have the opportunity or support they need to go fully through the identity-formation process, they are often blown about like a weathervane as they try to be the pastors each of their successive churches want them to be.

BECOMING A LEGITIMATE PASTOR

Forming a personally authentic pastoral identity is only part of living into a call to ministry. Flourishing pastors also formed pastoral identities and ways of enacting those identities in their ministries that were professionally legitimate. As I noted earlier, I use the term "professional" following its more historic definition as a group of individuals who undertake a vocation "based upon formal knowledge and trained skill, organized in a collegial or guild-like way, and carried on in the spirit of service." All professions have standards of appropriate training and personal development; codes of conduct; and norms about the dispositions, habits, knowledge, and ways of being that are central to the professional vocation. In this way the "profession" of clergy also has standards, codes, and norms. Becoming a legitimate pastor means being able to enact an authentic pastoral identity and ministry in ways that are also true to the profession.

Becoming Competent as a Pastor

One aspect of professional legitimacy is establishing competency as a pastor and moving toward mastery. Consider this quote:

I loved [my first sermons] and I felt like I really could do this. . . . More importantly, those sermons seemed to speak to my congregants. I could see that preaching the Word was touching them in important ways. I felt like I started to come into this [pastoral role] . . . and that it really could happen, that I could really be good at . . . I could claim preaching as part of my call.

Flourishing pastors want and need to be good at ministry. Earlier in the book I quote a pastor as saying, "We are all called to be excellent. No one is called to mediocracy." That quote reflects the deep commitment pastors have to create and lead fruitful ministries, and so becoming competent, and then aspiring to mastery, are central to being a real, bona fide pastor. Competency and mastery matter because living a calling means aspiring to be at their personal best. Many pastors spoke with disapproval of colleagues who did not appear to "really care about ministry" or "who just don't take the Gospel seriously." Competency is more than being good at one's work; it is seen as the right way to live out one's calling.

Pastors developed skill and, eventually, mastery in ministry work over time through a series of what I refer to as proficiency experiences. These are times in which a new pastor had the opportunity to perform some aspect of ministry work and then observe the results of these performances. The first several times a pastor preached are examples of proficiency experiences. The pastor preached and then tried to learn about how he or she performed in preaching. Most of the information about preaching performance came through the reactions of parishioners, but pastors often critiqued their own preaching. Sometimes they asked an experienced pastor to sit in on a sermon and then provide feedback. While it was important to have a personally authentic way to preach; that way of preaching also had to be effective. This was true for all core aspects of the pastoral role—preaching, teaching, care giving, administration, and so on—and also for their peripheral role features. Pastors sought proficiency experiences across the ministry activities—they wanted to be effective in all aspects of their ministry role. The goal of proficiency experiences was to confirm where they were competent and identify where they needed to develop competency. The goal is to be both personally authentic *and* to achieve excellence in ministry.

Pastors responded to successful proficiency experiences by claiming competency in that particular aspect of ministry, as the pastor I quoted earlier illustrates with the way he responded to his early experiences with preaching. One pastor said this about serving his first church: "I had done several hospital visits, and my congregants expressed that they appreciated those visits and I seemed to be helping them. Once learned I could do them well, I could kind of check the box on that one and then turn more of my attention to becoming a better preacher." By "checking the box," this pastor did not mean he would ignore hospital visits but rather that he knew he was competent in those visits and could devote additional time and work on other areas of his pastoral ministry.

Role Models

Unsuccessful proficiency experiences are seen by professionals as an impetus to develop the competency they lacked. One pastor shared, "I bombed my first sermons, so I worked hard, day and night to get better. Over time, I became good, at least good enough, at preaching." When pastors were uncertain about what constituted a credible role performance, they told of turning to role models from whom they could learn. Role models were experienced pastors, pastors who had already achieved mastery in one or more aspects of ministry. Role models provided examples of how to undertake different ministry activities and perform those activities well. For example, role models can describe the specific tasks a pastor should undertake when officiating at a funeral, good ways of preparing a sermon, and what to do during a hospital visit. In this way, role models helped pastors understand the "basics of good ministry work," as one pastor described it. The best role models created a safe space for the new pastor to admit their need to learn and improve. One pastor described her first experience with a funeral:

> I needed to ask questions that I felt were maybe a little weird, like should I walk with the body, or what kinds of things are helpful to say to a grieving family. It was so nice to be comfortable asking those question to [role model]. He told me he had the same questions during his first funerals. That opened things up and we had a great conversation about what we were really trying to do at a funeral.

Who do you turn to when you "bomb" your first sermons? You need a trusted role model to advise and guide you.

But even more, role models are seen as exemplars of the ideals of ministry, of what pastors should aspire to as they undertake different ministry activities. The steps or processes of officiating at a funeral are only part of what a pastor-in-formation needs to know. Even more important is what should a pastor aspire to when officiating at a funeral? What are the spiritual ideals a pastor should strive toward when undertaking the activities that constitute a good funeral? Beyond learning better ways of preparing a sermon, what makes for a "good" sermon? What are the spiritual ideals that a pastor should aspire to when creating and preaching a sermon? Role models are essential because they are living examples of excellence in ministry. In seminary, excellence in ministry is often a theoretical, abstract idea. Role models bring those ideals to life. What seems essential, then, is having at least one trusted role model. But a repertoire of different role models is best. The more role models and the more diverse they are, the richer a pastor's understanding of what excellence in ministry looks like and the more likely it is that the pastor can find his or her own way of achieving excellence in ministry.

Wise Guides

The best role models are wise guides—they provide personalized guidance to the pastor-in-formation, helping the pastor develop a sense of mastery and walking him or her through successful and unsuccessful proficiency experiences to help him or her learn. Wise guides are vulnerable—they share as much about their ministry struggles and failures as they do their ministry high points. One pastor shared this about her wise guide:

> She had a personality that was a lot like mine, and I could tell that her teaching style was a lot like mine would be . . . and she was very supportive of me, and she wanted to help me, but at the same time, she didn't just tell me, this is what you need to do. She let me figure things out on my own, try things. . . . She really shaped me, but she also helped me be myself.

Wise guides share richly detailed stories about their own experiences early in ministry, and they invite and listen to the stories of the pastor they are mentoring. Sharing stories creates space for the wise guide and the protégé to enter into ministry life together.

Perhaps most importantly, wise guides consistently affirm that the new pastor's personally genuine way of being a pastor is also a bona fide expression of pastoral ministry. This quote from one of our interviewees illustrates the power of affirmations from mentors: "When he [my wise guide] came to me with a spiritual challenge of his own, and he wanted my counsel and guidance, when he said I was his pastor, I knew my call was real. I knew I was really a pastor." Wise guides journey with pastors-in-formation, helping new pastors craft personally genuine pastoral identities, supporting new pastors in gaining mastery in ministry, and affirming the validity of pastors' calls to ministry.

The Fellowship of Pastoral Ministry

Affirmations from other pastors are also important. These affirmations come in a variety of ways, such as being welcomed by more senior clergy at annual pastoral gatherings or expressions of support and encouragement from other clergy. The essence of these affirmations from other clergy is being treated like a fellow pastor and thus being recognized as a bona fide pastor. This quote from a pastor illustrates the importance of being received into the fellowship of all clergy: "I could tell they thought I belonged with them, that they thought I was a pastor, too. That meant so much, to know that these great pastors saw me that way." Affirmations from other pastors validate that the newer pastor's unique expression of ministry—his or her personally authentic identity as a pastor—is also a bona fide, true to the pastorate identity. Statements such as "I knew I was really a pastor" capture this important experience of feeling that one's unique way of being a pastor is also consistent with what it means to be a real, true, legitimate pastor. Second, affirmations by other pastors convey a sense of solidarity with those who are similarly called. Statements like "I was one of them" illustrate this sense of being a full member of the company of pastors. Several pastors described this as feeling that they belonged in the brotherhood and sisterhood of all pastors.

Unfortunately, some clergy did not have this experience of belonging to the fellowship of all pastors. Women often experienced the opposite, a sense of being unwelcome or even ostracized by other pastors. As is the case in most professions, women continue to face challenges in being recognized as full members. Gendered norms certainly play a significant role. The "stained-glass ceiling" is very real, and many female pastors describe the insidious ways that male clergy signal they are not welcome. Pastors of color who serve in predominantly white denominations and congregations are also more likely to report feeling unwelcome or ostracized from the larger fellowship of pastors. This is one of the most powerful ways that clergy isolation is created, and the long-term impact on clergy wellbeing is likely very negative.

Clergy who go through alternative credentialing processes also often described feeling like "second-class pastors. The [ordained pastors] make it clear that we are not real pastors." Most denominations report that an increasing number of pastors are following these alternative credentialing processes, and this appears to be especially common among so-called second-career pastors. In our interviews, we found that many of the pastors who followed alternative credentialing processes reported feeling marginalized in their pastoral vocation. Several pastors described a "caste system" in the pastorate, in which only fully ordained pastors are granted the status of legitimate pastors.

Pastors who feel they are outsiders can carry on for a while, but over time, their outsider status will likely diminish their authenticity and thriving. This outsider status is particularly detrimental for newer pastors, in that it can create strong identity demands that keep these pastors from forming an authentic pastoral identity. Remedying this situation requires more than ceremonial expressions of inclusion; real cultural change is needed to recreate a fellowship that welcomes all persons who have properly achieved professional legitimacy.

Conferrals of Respect

Affirmations from church members are important as well. After all, pastors are called to serve their parishioners and need to know whether they are being fruitful servants. Conferrals of respect from church members are therefore very important. A pastor shared this story of how a conferral of respect shaped her identity: "I visited with them, and I celebrated communion with them, and I got ready to leave, and he grabbed my hands, and he looked me in the eye, and he said, 'You are my pastor; you are our church.' And it was so humbling and profound to me. . . . At that moment, I knew I really was a pastor." When church members convey that they regard the new clergy as a "real" pastor, it affirms that the new clergy's personally genuine identity is also a valid, bona fide expression of pastoral ministry.

Another pastor told of an older, taciturn man who was a longtime elder of the pastor's local church. For several months, this elder sat stoic in the pew Sunday after Sunday. The new pastor knew this elder was respected and influential in the church. The elder had seen many new pastors, so he had important experience and wisdom about how a new clergy could develop into an effective pastor. But each Sunday the elder left after worship ended without saying a word to the new pastor. But one Sunday, the elder approached the pastor: "He looked me in the eye, and I thought, 'Oh no! Here it comes.'" The elder, however, "had such a gentle look on his face" when he affirmed the new pastor's ministry: "You've got some growing to do, but you are doing fine." The new pastor was not seeking approval for egotistical or self-serving reasons; he wanted to know that his ministry was fruitful and that he was providing the kind of pastoral leadership that served his church well.

Sometimes pastors are admonished against seeking the approval of parishioners. This advice seems to be rooted in the assumption that approval seeking represents a weakness—"You should seek only God's approval," one new pastor was told. There may be some pastors-in-formation who do seek approval to prop up their self-esteem. Our research clearly shows, however, that affirmations from church members can and do serve a positive and important role in supporting pastoral formation. Churches can help newer pastors learn what fruitful ministry is like in action. Churches can help pastors translate the abstract, theoretical knowledge they acquired in seminary into actual ministry activities. And supportive churches can help newer pastors develop a pastoral identity that is both personally authentic and legitimate.

As you remember from Carolyn's story, females face challenges in ministry that males often do not experience. Validation as a female clergyperson is one that often surprises women as they develop professional identities. Although denominations have been ordaining women for decades and the number of women attending seminary has increased, the local church has been slower to experience women as clergy leaders. In the bubble of the seminary experience, in which women are around many other women in ministry, the thought that there would be pushback about their pastoral authority is late in being tested.

Carolyn's call was validated by her local church, her family, and church leaders, but it was in her first position as a solo pastor that she seriously questioned her call to ministry. She told the story of being in the restroom after worship one Sunday, when she was cornered by a female parishioner and challenged about her legitimacy as a female pastor. She had just preached her heart out, and she had had previous exchanges with this woman that seemed very positive. She was caught completely off-guard by the situation, and it really shook her. Unfortunately, this wasn't the only or the last time that another woman challenged her validity as a clergyperson. Of all the people she expected to question her call to ministry, she didn't expect it from female peers.

We learned from our research that women have found "work-arounds" in ministry that allow them to flourish or at least cope with the additional challenges they face. Carolyn was confident in her call to ministry and could describe it in various contexts. While she was happy and doing well in her local church context, she also could envision herself living out her call through other ministry situations. She described it as having plans A, B, and C. We came to describe this as flexibility in one's call to ministry. Her call was clear and specific: ministry in a local church was the best expression of her call. Yet she knew there were options if local church ministry no longer worked for her, especially if it interfered with her call to motherhood or if she felt undermined as a women in ministry. For example, plan B is to find a ministry role in hospice chaplaincy. She had explored how she might enter chaplaincy and was even seeking further CPE training to better prepare herself. Plan C was advocacy work through a local social service agency. Knowing that she had options to live into her call in another context empowered her to make choices at work that helped her to flourish. She was candid about what it would be like to face this choice—"The local church is where I feel most strongly called"—but she also knew the dark side of ministry work and was not willing to subordinate her family or let ministry damage her wellbeing or the wellbeing of her family.

Trends indicate that more pastors, including a growing number of younger and female pastors, are adopting flexible calls. We found strong evidence in our own research to support this shift. Some of this is also in response to changes in the religious nature of American culture. The rise of the "nones" and "done" are causing many younger pastors to look for and create ministries that are located outside of a local church context. The How We Gather project at Harvard Divinity School has mapped out this new ministry territory. Increasing pressures from inside denominations in response to declining membership has also been offered by many pastors as a reason to think about new ways to pastor. This pastor's description was echoed by many: "What really matters to [my denomination] is backsides in the pews and bucks in the offering plate. We act like we are still about loving people and helping them find the abundant life, but the new initiatives that come down from on high are all about keeping us from dying out." We heard similar sentiments across religious traditions. What was remarkable for us was that these pastors were in no way considering giving up ministry, but rather their responses were always to look for new places and new ways to be in ministry.

WHEN FORMATION IS INCOMPLETE

John's story illustrates what can happen when pastoral formation is incomplete. John imported his military identity of a leader into the church context. He knew how to be a good leader in the army and thought, therefore, that he would be effective in ministry. In some ways, his discernment process had been abbreviated as well. "I went into the military and just conformed to that role. In many ways, I never really got to know myself as a man, as a person." This meant that, when he went into ministry, he had insufficient self-knowledge to imagine himself as a minister. He tried for a long time to be the kind of leader he had been in the military but found himself overwhelmed. He longed for personal relationships, but his "command-and-control" style created barriers to creating friendships. And he scrambled to keep up with administrative responsibilities.

John faced a very "dark night of the soul. Well, it was a dark year or two." He courageously shared with some of the lay leaders of his church that he could not continue. One of those lay leaders, a physician, became a very important wise guide for John. Together they worked to help John rebuild his identity. "I got to know myself as a man. Then I could think about how God wanted me to be a pastor." Because this wise guide had seen John from the time he was a new pastor until he experienced burnout, he had deep experience with what had transpired. He was able to offer many important insights that helped John understand himself and his ministry better. That wise guide continues to be an important source of support: "I look out on Sunday and see him. . . . He loves me, he really does. To me, he is the best friend I have ever had."

John had to "face a lot of demons, some of them of my own making." His wife was an important part of this process as well. She and John spent many hours talking about ministry and life. "She knows me better than anyone; I think she knows me better than myself. She could speak truth to me, about who I was and what I was capable of doing." John shared that there were many sleepless nights as he wondered whether he would be able to return to full-time ministry. "I had to be honest with myself and honest with God."

He now has an authentic pastoral identity, and his church has asked him to remain their minister. He feels he is much more effective in ministry in part because he has clarity about his capabilities: "I ask for help when I need it." I interviewed John before and after he hit the wall and have seen him after he recovered. He is clearly much stronger and more confident with himself. His preaching is more compelling. He says he is a better leader, better pastor, better father, and better husband. His wife, children, and church agree.

SUMMARY

Becoming and being a pastor—the meanings embedded in that short phrase are deep. Becoming a pastor requires a profound transformation of one's identity, but it also requires staying true to oneself because being a pastor means, in part, being the pastor that only you can be. It requires self-integrity—having true self-knowledge that leads to balanced, secure self-worth as a person. On that secure foundation, a strong and clear pastoral identity can be formed. Being a pastor also requires being true to the pastorate and therefore forming an identity that is consonant with the ideals all pastors must aspire to embody. This "both-and" of being true to oneself and true to the profession requires deeper identity work that most working adults must undertake. Becoming and being a pastor is, in many ways, a lifelong journey of continuing to know oneself better and growing more fully into the pastor God has called you to be. As a pastor with more than fifty years of service told us, "There are always ways I can grow and change. They say you can't teach an old dog new tricks, but old pastors can and they must. God always has something new for us to do. If I remember that, and if I seek that out, then I can become a better pastor today than I was yesterday."

Chapter Seven

Social Support

The Bible is full of exhortations and encouragements about the importance of having strong, positive social relationships. Early in Genesis (2:18) we learn that God created us as social beings. In the beginning God commands, "It is not good for the man to be alone," and with Adam and Eve, the Bible begins a long series of stories—Abraham and Sarah, Ruth and Naomi, Abraham and Lot—about the importance of strong families, abiding friendships, and loving kindness toward others. The great leaders of the Bible relied on the support and care of others. Aaron held up Moses's arms when he grew tired. Elisha and his mentor, Elijah, were devoted friends. David's friendship with Jonathan strengthened his faith and his leadership. The fullness of our social nature is manifest in Jesus and his ministry: "My command is this: Love each other as I have loved you" (John 13:34).

Researchers agree. Studies conducted in more than forty countries around the world have found that positive, caring, nurturing relationships are among the most important conditions for wellbeing (Baumeister and Leary 1995; Berscheid 2010; Clark 2018). There are literally thousands of studies that show the many ways relationships are vitally important for our health and wellbeing. The need to be loved, accepted, and cared for is regarded by researchers as a fundamental human need. The absence of strong social support can have devastating effects on our health and wellbeing. Professor John Cacioppo (Hawkley and Cacioppo 2010) has studied loneliness, and his research shows how it leads to a variety of mental health challenges including depression, impairing a person's cognitive abilities, causing cognitive decline such as increased risk of Alzheimer's disease, and having a negative impact on physical health similar to heavy smoking and obesity. Dr. Cacioppo's research shows that one in four Americans suffers from loneliness—a level he describes as an epidemic.

Our research strongly concurs: strong, positive social relationships are vital for flourishing in ministry. We find that four kinds of social relationships are especially important: significant others (spouses, family, and friends), similar others (pastors, clergy, and other ministry workers), members of the local church a pastor is serving, and denominational leaders. Each of these different kinds of social relationships provides uniquely important forms of social support. All are necessary, but no single one is sufficient. I often use the term "ecosystems of wellbeing" to capture both the importance of each form of social support and the connections among these forms. Significant others, similar others, parishioners, and denominational leaders are important parts of the ecosystems in which clergy live and work.

Throughout our research, we have heard a lot from pastors, denominational leaders, and seminaries about clergy isolation. Isolation is usually described as being disconnected from other clergy, especially lacking friendships with other pastors. We find that this is, indeed, one important form of isolation, and we find that isolation from other pastors compromises flourishing in important ways. But there are other forms of isolation. One of the most common and pernicious forms is isolation from the members of the congregation the pastor serves. We sometimes refer to this as being lonely in a crowd because the congregation is ever present but there is a profound interpersonal gulf between them and the pastor. Many pastors have told us that they have been admonished against having "friendships" with their congregants. I have also read essays in leading religious publications that urge pastors against what one writer referred to as "relationships of mutuality." I find that phrase particularly evocative because, as I describe, one of the strongest and most consistent results from our research on social support is that a particular kind of mutuality is essential between pastors and their congregants. Strong, positive relationships between pastors and members of the church they serve is one of the single most important causes of flourishing. I certainly agree that appropriate relationships between pastors and their parishioners are also essential, and yet I also argue that, within the boundaries of the appropriate, there is room for mutual respect and care. I imagine there is a great deal of agreement between the perspective on pastor-parishioner relationships I describe and those of the thoughtful writers I have read.

In the sections of this chapter, I describe each of the four essential kinds of social relationships and explain how they impact a pastor's wellbeing. Keep in mind that these different social relationships form a social ecosystem. All are important. The absence of any one creates a particular form of isolation, and that isolation will almost certainly have negative effects on a pastor's wellbeing. In chapter 8 I describe how these different kinds of relationships and the social support they provide can combine to create a critical foundation for long-term flourishing, what I call a backstage.

SIGNIFICANT OTHERS

My first year as a thirty-something doctoral student was rough. I had left a job in which I was a manager to begin a role in which I was clearly at the bottom rung of the work hierarchy. To earn my graduate stipend, I spent many days photocopying research articles—a fair day's work, but I was having difficulty adjusting to the dramatic change in social status. I also felt completely lost in my graduate classes. I did not understand most of the terms I was reading, and trying to understanding even one research article seemed like an exercise in futility. I left campus on many of those early days feeling dejected, lost, and worried. But when I arrived at our small apartment, my boys (three and five years old at that time) ran to the door, excited to see me. They showed me that I was loved just for being me, no matter how I performed. My wife, Kim, sustained me, as she always has, with her abiding love, caring for me and providing a place to talk through the day and disconnect from my work. I am certain I would have quit the doctoral program had it not been for their sustaining care and love.

The term "significant others" is often misunderstood to mean only spouses or other romantic relationships. More properly a significant other is any person who currently or historically has a significant impact on our wellbeing, especially our emotional and spiritual wellbeing, and so significant others include other family members, close friends, wise elders, and other people with whom we have close and caring relationships. Notice in this definition that even past relationships with significant others are considered to be of importance to current wellbeing, which means that both good and bad relationships have a long legacy with our wellbeing.

Romantic love is a uniquely wonderful experience. As the research of John Gottman (Gottman and Silver 2014) shows, great marriages are of unique and special importance in a variety of ways and most certainly play a central role in the lives of many flourishing pastors. Unfortunately, pastors who experienced strained or poor marriages are likely to experience significant ill-being. When marriages are good, they are wonderful for wellbeing, but when they are not, they undermine wellbeing significantly. I want to emphasize that being single in no way destines a pastor to comprised wellbeing. Single pastors can and often do have strong relationships with significant others who help them to flourish.

Significant others provide several vitally important forms of social support. They provide emotional nurture and sustenance in the form of compassionate, agape love. Emotional support includes expressions of empathy, sympathy, and understanding. Significant others meet the powerful need we all have for unconditional positive regard, to be loved as we are and for who we are. Many researchers believe that this is the single most important kind of social support, and significant others are the primary source of agape love for most people, including most pastors.

Significant others are the go-to people for emotional support and sustenance in times of joy and sorrow. They can celebrate good times and sympathize in difficult times. Significant others are a safe refuge during any dark days of ministry, a source of warmth and compassion when life becomes difficult. They reduce the wear and tear and increase the joy of everyday life, and as a consequence they boost everyday happiness and foster higher levels of resilience among clergy. Significant others can help restore a sense of security, provide emotional comfort, and convey understanding and acceptance during times of adversity. They can help facilitate problem resolution, and they can reframe adversity as an opportunity for growth and development. When adversity has passed, significant others can restore our self-confidence and help us rebuild parts of ourselves and our lives that were damaged during the adverse experience.

Significant others are often the providers of a variety of forms of "instrumental" or "tangible" support, such as cooking meals, helping with family care responsibilities, and providing important material resources in times of need or emergencies. These kinds of tangible support are of central importance to our wellbeing. Pastors who have a warm and loving home to go to are much happier during their good days and much more resilient during their tougher days. One of the female pastors we interviewed described how nice it was to go home and "just be mom." She could take off her collar, put on her comfortable clothes, and enjoy being "mom, life partner to my husband, just being me. . . . They even pray before we eat!" All of those things and much more were a daily respite this pastor could rely on. A priest spoke about his running group, people who have known and loved him for years "as [Joe] and not as Father [Joe]." This group cared for one another during many difficult times, sharing in each other's joys and sorrows and providing a source of strength and reassurance.

Significant others have a profound influence on our self-integrity. They shape how we think about ourselves and our place in the world around us. Significant others know us for who we are, and they love us as we are. They care for us as *whole* persons; for pastors this means including and beyond their role as a clergy. This is especially true during early years in life, but significant others continue to shape our sense of self throughout our lifetimes. They shape our values and beliefs, the life goals we strive toward, and our basic orientations toward the world around us. My family was a key source of strength during my doctoral programs, in part because they buoyed my sense of personal value and worth. Likewise, significant others strengthen pastors' authenticity. As one pastor describes her family, "They love me whether I preach the best sermon ever or the worst sermon ever. Their love reminds me God is there for me, and they help me to keep trying." Pastors who have strong marriages, caring families, or deep friendships are much more likely to flourish because they have people who truly know them and truly care for them.

Another way that significant others impact self-integrity is through helping us grow, develop, and become better people. They can foster a desire to grow, encouraging us to take on new challenges and seek opportunities to stretch ourselves. They can help us see the opportunities for growth that exist in challenging situations. They can help us plan and strategize ways to grow, assist us during growth periods, celebrate our successes, and respond sensitively when we face setbacks. And they can foster what researchers refer to as the Michelangelo effect—they can help "sculpt" one another in such a manner as to bring each person closer to his or her best self. In chapter 3 I discussed the importance of having an integrated life narrative. Through the Michelangelo effect, significant others help us form a more integrated narrative, strengthen our true self-knowledge, and achieve greater self-integrity. Increasingly, I am convinced that strong relationships with significant others are essential for forming a quiet self. It is the rare person who can achieve true humility on his or her own.

Research studies demonstrate the health benefits of significant others (Pallini et al. 2018). Results from these studies show that people with strong and positive significant other relationships are also much more likely to engage in healthy behaviors and are less likely to engage in health-damaging behaviors such as poor eating habits, smoking, or abusing alcohol or drugs. These people also experience lower stress and better capacity to cope with any stress they do experience. They even get better rest and have more restorative sleep patterns.

Given the importance of significant others for clergy flourishing, it is important for pastors to have sufficient time in their daily lives to spend with those people who love and care for them. One of the ways that work-life imbalances create challenges to wellbeing is by limiting the amount of time pastors can spend loving and being loved by their significant others. Both quality time and quantity of time with significant others matters, for pastors and for these very important and very significant others.

SIMILAR OTHERS

Researchers use the term "similar others" to denote people who fill similar social roles or people who in other ways have significant life experiences that are similar to our own (Thoits 2011). No one really, for example, knows the challenges of being an only child like another only child. No one knows what it is really like to be the parent of a newborn unless he or she has parented a newborn. And no one knows what life as a pastor is really like unless he or she has been a pastor. The more similar another person is to us—similar in social roles, personality, life experiences, values and beliefs, life goals, and aspirations—the better. For example, a young female clergy would benefit immensely from the wise guidance of a more experienced female clergy, especially if they have similar personal characteristics, ministry orientations, and life experiences. Many of the young women clergy we interviewed spoke about the importance of being able to have conversations with other female pastors. They described the conversations as ranging from what to wear to particular events and activities—for example, full-immersion baptisms held at a river, prayer before Little League baseball games, dinner for a local community foundation—to sharing the joys and challenges of being a woman in ministry. The shared experience was itself a boost for their wellbeing. As I describe shortly, the advice and counsel they received from more experienced female clergy is also often a deep reservoir of encouragement and wisdom.

Similar others are uniquely positioned to provide several very important kinds of social support. First, because they have walked in our shoes, they can provide a special kind of emotional support: empathic understanding. They can truly commiserate. Similar others have firsthand, in-depth experience with similar events, so their care and comfort can reduce distress because they have experienced the same kinds of thoughts and feelings. They can help sustain hope in dark times and boost a sense of competence and self-worth during times when pastors feel challenged, misunderstood, or denigrated. Pastors can share their feelings—"ventilate" their experiences—with similar others without the fear of being sanctioned. Having "been there" in ministry themselves, similar others can understand expressions of distress and can validate the normalcy of another pastor's reactions. Rather than deny, criticize, or attempt to change those responses, similar others understand what is upsetting, worrisome, or threatening. Like all of us, pastors feel better simply because someone truly understands and validates their experiences. Research shows that the sheer presence of similar others—just being with them—can dramatically reduce both the physiological reactions to stress and adversity.

Second, similar others can be wise guides, providing expert, personalized advice and counsel. Wise guidance is much less about telling another pastor what to do and much more about journeying together in ministry. Similar others are in an ideal position to provide wise guidance. They can help another pastor accurately appraise a problematic experience and act as an expert "sounding board" to help think through what is happening. They are sources of good advice about how to handle ministry challenges. Similar others can also convey a deep sense of care and concern—they can "be there" in ways even significant others cannot because they know the experiences of life in ministry in a deeper and more personal way. The encouragement is more meaningful because they have lived through similar situations and truly know what the future is likely to hold.

Third, similar others can help sustain or restore another pastor's call to ministry. They are very important for helping other pastors sustain a positive pastoral identity. Similar others can express true companionship and convey to another pastor that he or she belongs in ministry and is regarded as a worthy pastoral colleague. They can boost another pastor's sense of self-esteem and self-efficacy in ministry, conveying a confidence that can help restore the pastor's own self-confidence. And for pastors who are struggling with their calls, similar others are indispensable for supporting self-integrity and, when needed, identity rebuilding and restoration. Similar others are often the best sources of positive help with striving to become more excellent as a pastor.

Last, similar others can be true role models, what we at the Flourishing in Ministry team call exemplars. Exemplars are pastors who are held in high esteem because of their commitment to and excellence in ministry. Exemplars can be emulated because there is clear evidence about the efficacy of their ways of doing ministry and being a pastor. They can inspire hope by fostering a positive sense of self in other pastors. Similar others are very positive and often very powerful sources of social comparison. They can help other pastors imagine their best selves; envision a better, brighter future; and ultimately flourish. And exemplars can provide personalized advice and counsel to other pastors, helping them to strive to become better pastors and better people.

LOCAL PARISHES AND CONGREGATIONS

As I note at the beginning of this chapter, one of the great open questions my team and I have found within the community of pastors is the question of whether pastors should be friends with members of their congregations. In many ways the different answers to this question pivot on how friendship is defined and what it means to create appropriate "boundaries" with members of one's local church. Most conversations around this question seek to understand how pastors, as the spiritual leaders of local church communities, can properly fill their ministry roles and also maintain their own wellbeing. I propose that, rather than blanket admonitions for or against friendships with members of the pastor's local church, we should explore the kinds of relationships that are beneficial to the pastor, church members, and ministry effectiveness and support pastors and parishioners in creating these kinds of relationships.

The evidence from our scientific research is conclusive: congregational support is essential. Pastors who report having better relationships with the congregation of the local churches they serve have much higher wellbeing. Part of this effect stems from the simple but profound fact that our wellbeing is impacted the most by those people with whom we interact the most. Again, this is a fundamental fact of human nature. The idea that we can somehow be impervious to the treatment of those people with whom we come into regular contact is fiction, and a potentially dangerous fiction when pastors are made to feel weak or otherwise flawed when they experience the negative effects of mistreatment from members of the churches they serve. It is striking how many pastors feel isolated from the members of their local churches. As one pastor put it, "I'm lonely in a crowd." Certainly, pastors are often responsible for some of this isolation, perhaps because of their own reluctance to engage with parishioners, perhaps because they have been trained to remain separate. Parishioners likewise often bear some responsibility, perhaps because of their own life challenges, because of misplaced expectations that pastors are self-sufficient, or simply because they overlook the very human needs their pastors experience. Clearly, creating positive relationships between pastors and parishioners is a joint responsibility and mutual privilege.

Another consistent finding in our research is that one of the most potent and damaging factors for pastors' wellbeing is mistreatment by parishioners. Harsh criticism, disrespect, rejection, and ostracism are, unfortunately, common for a significant portion of pastors. More than half of all pastors report at least one very serious incident of mistreatment in their years of service, and virtually all pastors can describe experiences of harsh criticism. Women and pastors of color are more often the target of mistreatment, and young pastors seem to be facing increasing incidents of harsh criticism and rejection. Mistreatment by even one church member can be damaging, but certainly the greater the incendence, the stronger the negative impact on a pastor's wellbeing. Mistreatment seems to usually go unaddressed by other parishioners, and yet it is a whole-church problem. I urge parishioners to step in when they see their pastors mistreated. At the very least, they should be active in supporting the pastor but I urge them to intervene to address the mistreatment when and where opportunities arise.

In our research surveys when we asked pastors to rate the quality of the relationships they have with the congregation of the churches they served; we asked them questions like these: To what extent do members of the congregation you serve

- help you better understand yourself and gain insights about yourself?
- understand and know you and accept you for who you are?
- show concern for you and truly care about you?
- support you when you face challenges and difficulties?
- help you grow and develop as a pastor?
- help you grow and develop as a person?

Pastors who report higher levels of support from their congregations on questions like these have much higher levels of wellbeing across all four dimensions. The same is as true for new pastors as it is for pastors with ten or twenty or thirty years of service. It is the same for pastors regardless of age, gender, race, or ethnicity. It is true for pastors in Mainline, Pentecostal, Evangelical, and Roman Catholic traditions. In other words, for all kinds of pastors, those who report stronger and better social support from their congregations on dimensions like those represented here also have much higher levels of daily wellbeing, resilience, authenticity, and thriving. Pastors who experience social support from their congregations are much more likely to flourish.

What kinds of social support can parishioners provide? First, at a minimum, local churches should create what researchers refer to as mutually responsive relationships, in which each member effectively strives to understand, accept, and care for the other members. Said differently, pastors should be a part of the network of care that includes all church members. Each member, including the pastor, should feel respected by others. Each member's dignity should be honored, sustained, and preserved, which requires consistent and active displays of respect, of being honored, and of being cared for. Expressions of gratitude, gestures of positive regard, acts of kindness, and expressions of care and concern—these are important for sustaining the wellbeing of all church members, including the pastor.

Second, parishioners should be positive ministry partners. Shared ministry values, shared commitment to ministry goals, and shared engagement in ministry activities are all important for effective ministry, but they are also important forms of social support for all ministry workers, including the pastor. Toiling alone in any enterprise is difficult, and it is especially challenging when one is working solo in a group. Collaboration and other forms of ministry partnership are psychologically encouraging and energizing. Pastors need people they can count on to get work done, to share the workload, and to experience the joy of working together to achieve important objectives. Sharing work gets more work done, alleviates burdens of coworkers, and reduces everyone's overall workload.

Third, research now shows that responding well to stress and adversity requires a communal response. There are a variety of mechanisms through which communal responses are more beneficial than individual action: obstacles seem less onerous, collaboration creates more effective problem solving, mutual support and commiseration buffer negative effects, help from others ensures needs are met, and people feel loved and cared for.

Should pastors be friends with parishioners? Jackson Carroll (2006), in his book *God's Potters*, summarizes his insights about how social relationships impact clergy and their leadership by emphasizing that, "despite their potential for mischief, friendships with parishioners and non-parishioners, as well as with fellow clergy are essential for a pastor's mental and spiritual well-being—as long as they have clear boundaries. Without them, the ministry can be lonely and debilitating experience." I agree. We have heard from a significant number of pastors who have had close friendships with select members of the churches they served. Most pastors described the many rich and significant benefits they have experienced through such relationships. Most of these pastors described the careful way they entered those friendships, and they emphasized that such friendships are not appropriate nor have they been available in every church they served. We have also heard stories about friendships that went bad, and those stories show that the cautions offered about pastor-parishioner relationships should be heeded. As Carroll notes, mischief is possible in all forms of relationships, and so proper relational "boundaries" are important for all of them, including friendships with parishioners.

As I have described, however, there is more to congregational care than friendships. To flourish, pastors need to experience at least a minimal level of respect, care, concern, and positive regard from most members of their congregations. Those who do not will face severe challenges to their wellbeing. As inherently social beings, most of us cannot flourish unless we experience the minimum social support requirements: respect, care, concern, and compassion from those people with whom we interact on a regular basis. Let me emphasize this point: most pastors will not flourish unless they experience these minimum requirements for flourishing. Local churches must be active supporters of pastors and of the ministries that pastors lead.

DENOMINATIONAL LEADERS

There is a very large and growing body of research on leadership, including the impact of leaders on the wellbeing of their followers. This research shows that two characteristics of leaders and leadership are consistently related to high follower performance and high follower wellbeing. The first is authentic leadership, which is a pattern of ethical leader behavior that fosters an open, transparent, and caring environment. Authentic leaders are self-aware and humble. Because of this, they seek out and rely on followers' input. The second is referred to as transformational leadership. It comprises conveying to followers that they are cared for by the leaders and then inspiring followers to perform beyond expectations while transcending self-interest for the good of the organization. Denominational leaders can play similar roles in religious organizations. We find that pastors who report experiencing authentic and transformational leadership from denominational leaders are more likely to flourish.

We distinguish between close and distant leaders. A close leader is a pastor's immediate supervisor, the person next in line in the organizational hierarchy. This is often the leader of the pastor's district, synod, state, or region. Distant leaders hold the most senior or "highest" positions in the denomination: members of the council of bishops and general board and executive council are examples. These leadership positions vary considerably by polity, but even in denominations with so-called congregation-based polity, there are clergy who serve the role of leaders. Often in this context large-church pastors play a role very similar to that of a closer or distant leader.

Close leaders can have a significant impact on the wellbeing of clergy, for better and for worse. At their best, closer leaders can be similar others—brothers and sisters in ministry who can offer care, support, and wise guidance. Sometimes, however, they are seen as performance monitors. Their roles may be structured in such a way that the close leader is truly a supervisor rather than a friend in ministry. When, however, close leaders are able to be friend, wise guide, or exemplar, they can be significantly beneficial to pastors. And such close leaders are important resources for sustaining wellbeing.

Distant leaders serve as living embodiments of the values and beliefs of the religious tradition. The ways they act, the decisions they make, and the manners in which they interact with other pastors are all signs of what truly matters in the denomination. Therefore distant leaders who exemplify the true values and best traditions of the religious tradition can be inspiring to other pastors. However, when they are viewed as serving other interests than those of the denomination, they can undermine the morale of other pastors. We heard many stories of the profoundly positive experience pastors have when they meet an admired distant leader. Such meetings can inspire pastors and reinvigorate their calls. We have also heard stories of senior leaders who seem preoccupied with "the numbers" or with advancing their own careers. These distant leaders create negative ripple effects of dissatisfaction and discord.

Leadership matters for wellbeing. Our research and the larger body of scholarship consistently show the best leaders are those who focus first on the wellbeing of their followers and second on "performance." As denominations experience significant declines in membership, we hope the leaders of those organizations can continue to be the authentic, transformational leaders their denominations and their pastors need.

SUMMARY

We all live in a social ecosystem of wellbeing. Our wellbeing is connected in deep and profound ways to the wellbeing of others, including our families, colleagues, neighbors, and congregations. Pastors and denominational leaders often speak about the importance of "self-care." Each of us certainly does have important responsibilities to ensure we are healthy and flourishing. But we are also responsible for each other. The term "self-care" does not draw attention to the ways we impact each other's wellness and wellbeing. We need both "self-care" and "other care" because we all live in ecosystems of wellbeing. For pastors, these ecosystems include significant others, similar others, members of their churches, and denominational leaders. Pastors may have other important sources of social support, but the Flourishing in Ministry research has conclusive evidence that each of these four kinds of social support are essential for the flourishing of pastors.

Chapter Eight

The "Stages" of Ministry

I want to build on the last chapter by describing how social support can foster wellbeing across all four dimensions. It distills several key insights from our research and highlights, especially, an important way that pastors, churches, and denominations can create ministry contexts in which pastors will flourish. I build this around a metaphor of ministry life as a theater. Jackson Carroll (2006) uses this metaphor in his book on clergy leadership, and I want to build on his ideas here,

I remember the very first time I saw live theater. I was on a high school trip to New York City. Part of our itinerary was to see Carol Channing in *Hello Dolly*. I expected to be bored, but instead I was enthralled. We had great seats, very close to the stage, and I was fascinated with the changing of the sets, the way microphones were hidden around the stage, and the way the actors looked from close view. I could see how hard they were working, but Ms. Channing was so delightful and convincing that I found myself convinced that she was enjoying herself as much as I was. I caught glimpses of the back stage during set changes, and I wondered who was back there and what was going on. Even with those brief glimpses, I could tell that the back stage was important for supporting everything that happened on stage.

The metaphor of a theater is very useful for understanding many aspects of flourishing in ministry, and it is especially helpful for describing the role of social support in wellbeing. The front stage is where performance happens. The back stage is the place to support and nurture great front stage performance. And the off stage is a place to step away from performance roles and engage other parts of life. Let's begin with the metaphor of the front stage—the place where the action happens.

GREAT PERFORMANCES
HAPPEN ON THE FRONT STAGE

Any time we enact an important social role—pastor, parent, friend, professor—we operate on a set of expectations about the things we should do and say. When I am enacting the role of professor, for example, there are certain ideals of being a professor I aspire to embody, including showing compassion to my students and guiding them to learn and grow as persons. These ideals also include expectations about proper conduct—I certainly do not say and do the same things when I am with my students that I would when I am with family and close friends. Each of the important social roles we fill has a set of expectations about the kinds of behaviors, goals, responsibilities, and interaction styles that are proper. We expect professors to do certain things and act in certain ways. These expectations shape the social role.

There are expectations about the pastoral role. Preaching, teaching, and caring are nearly universal parts of the pastoral role. There are also expectations about the way pastors should *be*. Pastors are not only expected to do certain things, but they are also expected to have a certain demeanor, certain ways of interacting with people, and perhaps even certain ways of speaking. Some of these expectations are proper and reasonable—they form the ideals that all pastors should aspire to enact. For example, there are common understandings of what excellent ministry is and what kinds of things most pastors should do to create excellent ministries. But other expectations can be inappropriate and unduly constrain pastors into an overly tight box of unreasonable demands. In chapter 5 I referred to these improper expectations as identity demands. Most often, identity demands are made by members of the pastor's local church, but sometimes demands arise from the culture of the pastor's denomination. Examples of identity demands abound: lay leaders pressure a pastor into trying to become a charismatic preacher, yet the pastor knows that is not one of his gifts. After preaching about the importance of welcoming everyone into the church, including the homeless veterans who live in the neighborhood, a new pastor receives feedback from his regional leader to "dial back the political rhetoric" and preach "happy sermons." Or a female pastor is consistently told by lay leaders that she should be more "commanding" and "authoritative," which seems to be code for "be a man."

When pastors are compelled to try to meet these unreasonable demands, they experience what researcher Patricia Hewlin (2009) calls facades of conformity. Pastors try to meet the demands—to "fake it until you make it," as several pastors described it—but they experience stress and internal tension because they sense that faking it will not work. They cannot, as one pastor put it, "be what God did not make me to be." Sadly, under continued pressure from his congregation, this pastor continued the façade until he finally left ministry. "I just couldn't take it anymore." His denominational leaders were surprised. He had been identified as a "rising star" and was expected to eventually be a pastor at a large, flagship church. Unlike actors in a theater who must pretend to be the character, pretending in a social role can be onerous and detrimental. It creates stress and strong internal tensions. We cannot continue pretending for too long without it damaging our wellbeing.

Authentic front stage performances most certainly must fit or fill the social role—they are not full-on improvisations to do whatever feels good to the pastor. There are ideals of pastoral leadership that ministers should properly aspire to fulfill. But our research shows that, when pastors can be more authentic—when they have the skills to perform well in their current ministry role and when they have the latitude to appropriately express their unique call and personality in their ministry work—they are both more effective and much more likely to flourish.

THE VITAL IMPORTANCE OF A GOOD BACK STAGE

Sustaining excellent, authentic front stage performances requires what sociologist Erving Goffman (1956) describes as a back stage, the place in which actors can drop their front stage roles, "forgo speaking in lines and step out of character." When actors go into a good back stage, they can rest and relax. They are in a safe space in which they are free to express things that cannot or should not appear on the front stage. A good back stage is separate from the front stage: other actors are present, but the audience is not. Here actors can step out of character without fear of disrupting the performance or unsettling their audience. It is where actions, ideas, and facts that should be suppressed on the front stage can be shared. In our research we find that great back stages are essential for fostering excellent, authentic pastoral ministry and for supporting and sustaining flourishing. Three important supportive activities happen for pastors in a good back stage.

The Characteristics of a Good Back Stage

A good back stage provides a place to review and improve front stage performance. It is a place to unpack what happens on the front stage, to review what went well and what did not go well, and to explore what led to a good or poor performance. It is a place to practice and sharpen skills for the front stage. It is a place to rehearse future performances, a place to improvise and generate new ideas for the front stage. One pastor described "bombing his first sermons" and said he felt lost about how to improve his preaching. Thankfully, he had a good back stage: he was part of a group of pastors who had attended seminary together and continued to gather regularly to talk about ministry life, share joys and sorrows, and support each other. He could share his experiences with this group and get practical, helpful advice about how to improve. He practiced preaching in front of this group. Over time, that advice and his own determined efforts helped him to become "at least a decent preacher. I'm never going to knock their socks off, but at least I am competent." My team and I have learned that pastors are more willing to share their ministry "failures" than they are to celebrate their ministry successes. A good back stage will encourage proper celebrations, what researchers call "capitalizing on the good." Studies show that when we share about personal positive events, we gain additional benefits from this sharing as do those close others that we share with. Think of capitalizing on the good as very similar to counting your blessings. It is sharing, with gratitude and modesty, how you are participating in creating effective ministry. To be sure, God is at work as well, but so are you. Celebrations build self-efficacy and self-confidence, strengthen ministry capabilities, and boost wellbeing across all four dimensions.

Second, a good back stage provides support and care for pastors. It is a place of emotional sustenance, where genuine expressions of caring and understanding are offered. Good performances are honored, bad performances are commiserated with, and pastors receive the nurture and support they need to sustain their wellbeing and to return again to the front stage. Here each pastor is shown that they truly matter to other people. Others act purposefully to help sustain each pastor's sense of efficacy and self-worth. Pastors are accepted within a network of caring others. Pastors often spend a great deal of time supporting and caring for others. This is, of course, an important part of pastoral ministry. What is often missing among pastors is receiving the care and support that they need. The pastor's family is an important source of this support and care. Other pastors can be a particularly strong source of back stage support and care. They are what I referred to in chapter 7 as similar others. Other pastors can commiserate well because they, too, know what it is like to be a pastor. They have faced similar challenges and obstacles, so their expressions of fellowship and support are genuine. Other pastors can provide support that is tailored to a pastor's unique needs and specific situation. There is a special depth of care we experience from someone who has similar life and ministry experiences to our own. Other pastors in the back stage help pastors adopt effective strategies for coping with the normal stresses that are part of the front stage. In the back stage a distressed pastor can receive information and personal advice to help him or her resolve problems or adapt to challenges. This kind of coping assistance is a stress buffer because—when successful—it quite literally lessens situational demands and helps ameliorate pastors' emotional reactions to those demands. One pastor's sentiments about the benefits of his friendships with other pastors reflects what we heard from many other pastors: "They just get me, as a person and a pastor. They are there for me, always."

A good back stage helps pastors grow and develop as persons and as pastors. This includes what is commonly referred to as "accountability." Typically, accountability means someone helping us understand where we are falling short of our ideals, situations in which we have not acted at our best, and areas of our lives where we can and should strive to be better. What is often missing from conversations about accountability, however, is the essential foundation that makes effective accountability possible. There are quite literally hundreds of research studies that confirm that, without these critical relational building blocks, most of us will react negatively to bad news delivered by another person. We will either become defensive, protesting that we have been misunderstood and unfairly judged, or dismissive, discounting the credibility of the information and perhaps even the integrity of the messenger. Effective accountability occurs when we really listen and react positively to tough news delivered to us by another person. Effective accountability happens when we take news about personal deficiencies or moral lapses to heart and become fully committed to the hard work and difficult changes required to make things better.

To be truly effective, accountability requires that our relationship with the messenger be firmly founded on trust. Trust is critically important because effective accountability is built on a willingness to be vulnerable to another person, a readiness to really listen to unpleasant news about what we are doing or how we are living, and the motivation to engage in the sometimes difficult work required to become a better worker or a better person. Trust is a marvelous resource because it grows with use. We begin by trusting someone in small things, and as he or she honors our trust, we can rely on him or her for more important things. At the same time, when others honor our trust, they come to rely on us, and in so doing their trust in us grows. To trust someone, we must have confidence in their integrity, benevolence, and abilities. Integrity is our perception that another person acts consistently on a set of moral principles that we endorse and value. To trust another, we must see them as a person who strives to live with virtue and honor. Benevolence exists when we believe that the other person cares about us and is deeply motivated by a desire to help us. Ability refers to our confidence in a person's knowledge, skills, wisdom, and insights. You might view me as a person of integrity and benevolence, but you cannot trust me to do brain surgery because I have no training in (and probably no talent for) neurosurgery.

Effective accountability starts when we foster a trust-based relationship with another person, and over time, we learn we can rely on their wisdom, insight, and help. As trust grows, so does our willingness to really listen to our trusted partner's perspective and to act on what we hear. As trust grows, so does our willingness to become open to our trusted partner's candid advice about changes we should consider making as we strive to reach our full potential. If we really want to hold others accountable, we start by holding ourselves accountable to building trust with those people. Beginning there not only creates the possibility for true accountability, but it also usually invites others to actively seek it with us.

THE RIGHT PEOPLE FOR A GOOD BACK STAGE

Having the right people in a back stage is essential. Significant others, such as family and friends, can be helpful, but most important are *similar others*, people who have experienced the front stage and, ideally, people who have filled similar roles themselves. Similar others can provide uniquely important social support. First, while significant others can *sympathize*, similar others can *empathize*. Because of their previous experience on the front stage, similar others have an in-depth understanding of the many dimensions and nuances of the front stage. They can really imagine what a stressful or challenging situation is like. It is such a relief to be understood by someone else, to have someone who can truly commiserate with and validate our experiences. Similar others can grasp the full meaning and implications of the stressful situation that another actor faces. This capacity for empathic understanding provides distressed actors with opportunities to ventilate their feelings and worries with less fear of criticism or sanction. Sometimes getting something "off your chest" is all a person needs to be able to perform well again on the front stage. Researcher Peggy Thoits (2011) refers to this as "ventilation and validation" and she notes that it can reduce experiences of stress and restore wellbeing.

Second, similar others can provide valid feedback about frontstage performance. They can provide expert critiques because they really know what kinds of performance are best and what is required to get those best performances. They can reinforce other actors' strengths and provide real insights into opportunities for improvement. In most cases, the evaluations and appraisals of similar others are much more accurate than those of significant others or people from the audience. Similar others can provide personalized advice and counsel, tailoring their support and help to a particular actor and to the role that actor is striving to fill.

Third, similar others can provide what Thoits (2011) calls active coping assistance to help other actors deal with stressors and crises. Because they are experienced experts, similar others are in a position to understand and make more accurate evaluations and appraisals of the situation. They can provide help that is closely tailored to the specific nuances of a particular problematic situation. And their commiseration can dampen another actor's despair by lessening situational demands and negative feelings directly.

Last, wise and experienced similar others—we call them wise guides rather than mentors—can serve as role models to be learned from and emulated. Wise guides have their own repertoire of effective problem-solving strategies to share and their own experiences from which other actors might learn. They can inspire hope and help other actors find again the meaning and purpose of their front stage. Wise guides can help other actors imagine a better future and a better self toward which they can aspire. They share their own experiences of the highs and lows of the front stage. By describing their own journeys, wise guides provide a way for other actors to reflect on their own journeys. They are mentors but also much more. Wise guides are friends and companions, caregivers and care receivers, fellow travelers on a journey through life.

TRULY GETTING OFF STAGE

The off stage is the place where actors are not involved in the performance in any way. In the off stage, actors are not doing frontstage things, nor are they thinking about being on the front stage. In a good off stage, actors are not concerned about performing and, in fact, they are not thinking about the theater. Here people can engage parts of themselves that do not or cannot appear in the front stage. Actors can be something other than actors: they can be spouses, parents, athletes, hobby enthusiasts, and even couch potatoes. For pastors, the back stage is where they can be more than a pastor. In the off stage, they can temporarily set aside pastor responsibilities and pastor ways of being. They can express authentic dimensions of themselves that are not part of their role as pastor. One key to a good off stage is the opportunity to temporarily forget about the front stage. Pastors need time to be truly off the ministry clock. They need, for example, to know they will not be called for an emergency—someone else will attend to immediate care needs. In the off stage, someone else prays before a meal. The pastor is treated as a person with his or her own valid wants, needs, and desires.

SUMMARY

In our research we found, unfortunately, that many pastors do not have a back stage. Often it is simply that pastors are not given the time they need to create and sustain a back stage. For example, daily ministry tasks leave little time to develop positive, supportive relationships with other pastors. We found that in some situations local church leaders did not endorse their pastor taking time away from work for "personal" issues. Prescribed back stages (for example, mentor-matching programs or geographically oriented pastor "support" groups) often do not work because back stages require people we trust, people enough like us to understand our experiences and different enough to help understand those experiences and grow beyond them. These kinds of relationships form over time, and they often begin from having the right opportunities—a kind of holy serendipity—to meet the people who can become friends and, eventually, back stage partners. Sometimes denominational issues can challenge a back stage. It is hard, for example, to share freely with someone who in the future might be your boss.

Forming and sustaining a good back stage is a group effort, one that certainly requires the involvement of pastors themselves and also the active and strong support of both local church leaders and denominational leaders. The myth of self-care may be creating cultural norms or organizational policies that impede or discourage pastors from forming a back stage. Workload, geographic isolation, or limited resources can make it difficult for pastors to actively participate in a back stage. This is one area of wellbeing where local churches and denominations can play a significant role in helping create opportunities that pastors can then act on.

Chapter Nine

A Way Forward

This chapter provides three roadmaps about how to develop specific interventions to enhance and sustain flourishing: one for pastors, a second for local churches, and a third for judicatories and denominations. Rather than offer specific prescriptions, these roadmaps provide individual clergy with important principles to guide them in selecting or developing wellbeing practices that are specific to their lives and ministry contexts. Similarly, the roadmap for churches, judicatories, and denominations provides evidence-based principles to guide leaders as they design and implement new initiatives to support wellbeing among their member clergy. I provide short case studies to illustrate how these principles have been used by individual pastors, churches, and denominations. I end the book with ideas about how pastors and denominations might use insights from the Flourishing in Ministry project to create communities of flourishing in both their local churches and in the towns and cities that are home to their churches.

For both individuals and organizations, it is important to remember that wellbeing includes all four building blocks. To flourish, we need to experience everyday happiness, have high resilience; experience self-integrity; and find meaning, purpose, and positive connectedness in all of the important spheres of our lives. Many people overlook everyday happiness. The days and weeks run together in a blur of unhappiness. Taking time to map our days can help us understand how to boost our daily happiness. Resilience helps us deal with the challenging days, but even more important, it helps us adapt and grow ever closer to our full potential. It is also essential for maintaining the other three domains. Self-integrity helps us feel like whole, valuable, worthy people and allows us to make meaningful contributions in our work and lives. And thriving helps us know life has meaning, that our lives have purpose, and brings us that essential care, respect, and love we need from others. They are the four building blocks of flourishing. It is also important to remember the ecosystems that underlie the roadmaps I present here. Another way of saying this is that the roadmaps overlap. Flourishing requires the concerted and sustained effort and attention of individual pastors, local churches, *and* denominations. These three are critically important elements of the ecosystem of flourishing.

ROADMAP FOR PASTORS

Small Steps, Step Back, Step Together

There are three essentials for boosting and sustaining wellbeing: small steps, step back, step together. The first essential, *small steps*, refers to the fact that simple practices that often take just a few minutes add up over time to big changes in wellbeing. This is true for the ways that wellbeing improves, as well as how it declines. Rarely, for example, does someone become burned out because of one event. Burnout happens one stressful event at a time, and many of these events are small and therefore easy to overlook and forget. Similarly, improvements in wellbeing rarely happen in one big leap forward but instead result from intentionally engaging in the types of wellbeing practices that will create small steps forward. This is great news because it means that improving wellbeing does not require hours of time, nor does it require wholesale changes in life or work. For example, a large and rapidly growing body of research shows that engaging in some form of contemplative or mindfulness practice for just five minutes on most days can, over time, improve daily wellbeing and boost resilience. All that is necessary is to find a practice that helps you quiet your mind, calm your body, and focus your attention on something positive. So five minutes of lexio divina or singing a praise hymn or sitting quietly in the presence of God is not only a good spiritual discipline, but it is also a wise wellbeing practice.

There are a wide variety of small-step wellbeing practices, which means each person can find something that will work for him or her. Because they are *small* steps, these wellbeing practices will fit into our already-busy lives. Table 9.1 describes the kinds of practices that scientific evidence, including our research with clergy, has shown are highly effective small steps that will improve and sustain each of the four dimensions of wellbeing. There are seven kinds or categories of practices described in the table, and the dimensions of wellbeing that each category impacts is also listed. You can adjust any of these to fit your own style, preferences, or ministry context. You can also use this guide to evaluate new wellbeing practices that you might read about in the media or find on the internet. You can even try creating your own wellbeing practice using the description and examples as a guide.

My team and I have created a website and an application for your smartphone or tablet to help you find the right small steps for you. You can learn more about these resources at: www.flourishinginministry.org. I encourage

Table 9.1. Wise "Small Step" Wellbeing Practices

Description of Strategy	Wellbeing Dimensions Strengthened
Tranquil (calming) practices foster openness to the present moment by gently acknowledging and letting go of distractions; enhance capacity to experience calm thoughts and peacefulness in the present moment.	Happiness Resilience
Receptive (appreciative) practices build capacity to observe one's thoughts and feelings from detached, big-picture perspective; enhance awareness of how the external environment is affecting one's thoughts and feelings; foster capacity to fully acknowledge (for example, radical and courageous acceptance) and detach from ("letting go") painful experiences.	Happiness Resilience Authenticity
Engaged (active) practices promote and strengthen positive, meaningful, goal-oriented action; strengthen and support capacity to pursue personally valued activities in daily life; motivate positive personal change encourage use of positive coping and self-regulation.	Happiness Thriving
Joyful (encouraging) practices boost and sustain optimism about oneself and one's life; strengthen the ability to maintain hope in difficult situations; foster experiences of awe, wonder, and inspiration; promote daily positive experiences and minimize daily negative experiences.	Happiness Resilience Thriving
Confident (self-assuring) practices support development of self-integrity (self-worth, self-confidence, self-compassion); promote competency/mastery in major areas of life activity; foster authenticity and ability to express preferred self in all major areas of life; nurture quiet self.	Authenticity Thriving
Dedicated (spirited) practices foster development and expression of core commitments (clearly articulated and strongly embraced life values, personal passions, moral frameworks); promote and sustain meaning and purpose in all areas of life; build and sustain membership in communities dedicated to living out shared commitments.	Resilience Authenticity Thriving
Connecting (relational) practices promote and sustain strong, mutually supportive social relationships in all major areas of life; encourage development of positive friendships (companionate-love relationships) in all major areas of life activity; build a positive back stage.	Resilience Authenticity Thriving

you to select one and commit to trying it at least five of the next seven days. If you do not like that practice, select another and give it the five-day trial. The goal of the five-day trial is to find a small step that you can keep taking. It is unlikely that you will notice significant changes in your wellbeing over those five days, but changes are occurring. Remember, there is scientific evidence that shows these wellbeing practices are the kinds of small steps that will help build and sustain your wellbeing.

The second essential for building and sustaining wellbeing is *step back* from the flow of life to gain perspective on your good days and bad days. Step back is simply being more aware of the highs and lows of your daily life. What are the positive activities, events, and social exchanges at work and at home? What are the stressful tasks, experiences, and interactions in your ministry life and your home life? We often lose track of the highs and lows of life as the days flow all too quickly past us. There is a quick way to illustrate this: Can you remember what you had for your evening meal last night? Can you remember your evening meal from a week ago? A month ago? Most of us cannot, unless we stick to the same menu week to week. This illustration is simply meant to encourage you that, if you cannot remember, you are like most people. Stepping back is a way to keep track of what happens. Once you identify what kinds of activities, events, and interactions naturally boost your daily wellbeing and those that diminish it, you can start to find ways of taking small steps to make your days better.

A simple way to step back is a wellbeing practice I call Map Your Day. It is simple, it doesn't take much time, and it can improve your wellbeing significantly. Get a pad of paper or notebook to use as something like a daily diary. Or you can also use our mobile app, which has Map Your Day built into it as one wellbeing practice. Either way, it is a simple process. At the end of a day, just quickly decide whether that day was a good day or a bad day. Try not to overthink it, and try to be as candid with yourself as you can. You are not whining or being ungrateful on the bad days; you are having a very normal human experience. Then draw either a smiley face or a frowny face to indicate what kind of day it was for you. If you do not like faces, use some symbol or number to record your daily wellbeing on that day. Then, in a few sentences, write about one high point from that day and one low point. These highs and lows can be about something you did, an event, a social interaction—whatever comes to mind as something that stood out for you as a high and a low. Try to Map Your Day for at least two weeks. Then look back over your daily record. Look for patterns in the high points—what are the common elements? Look for patterns in the low points—what consistent patterns do you see? Now look at the good days: What were the highs and lows? What made those days good? Then look at the bad days, searching for what you can learn about what caused your daily wellbeing to be lower. Once you identify the high points and low points of your days, you can find ways of taking small steps to bring in more highs and mitigate the lows.

That last essential is *step together*. Whenever possible, join with at least one other person to either support you in taking your small steps or to take small steps together. A great place to start stepping together is to have members of your family or your coworkers map their days. I did this with my research team. We found some common high points and low points, which empowered us to make changes that benefitted everyone. We also found some unique highs and lows, but even so we still found ways to work together to create more good days for everyone. One of my low points is administrative paperwork, which several of my team members enjoy and are quite adept at performing. By surfacing this low point experience with my team, I was able to find help that alleviated this low-point activity. It was a win-win for me and those team members. You might find a group of other pastors who would be willing to map their days. Sharing your ministry highs and lows in a circle of peers could create opportunities to support each other and yield new insights about how each pastor can enhance the highs of ministry life and deal more effectively with the lows. Stepping together is so important that I dedicated two chapters to describing the ways that social support and a good backstage contribute to wellbeing.

I encourage pastors to use the resources provided by their denominations or church networks. Most of these organizations provide pastors access to a set of employee assistance programs (EAPs) that are usually designed by professionals and can therefore provide high-impact resources that can be very helpful for boosting and sustaining wellbeing. EAPs are also often subsidized or free, so they can be a very cost-effective resource. But they are often underutilized—a treasure trove of wellbeing resources that are used by too few pastors. Use table 9.1 to help you select the EAPs that might be best for you. Finally, there are many highly qualified experts—therapists, counselors, life coaches, and more—who can provide personalized guidance, especially during difficult times. In our research we found that, for many flourishing pastors, seeing one of these experts on a regular basis is one of their core wellbeing practices.

Addressing Clergy Burnout

One of the primary causes of burnout is chronically low daily wellbeing. Pastors who have more good days than bad days also have higher resilience, while those who have too many bad days are much more likely to have low resilience and, eventually, to "hit the wall," to use John's term. So one way to boost resilience is to create more good days. Using the Map Your Days process takes a few small steps to create more good days. Your daily experiences, some of your important life dynamics, will show up in that map, but it may helpful to focus on specific kinds of dynamics. You can map work-life or work-family dynamics as well. When are things tense and difficult between work and the rest of your life? When is there a nice rhythm between the two, when everything seems balanced and smooth? Map the patterns in your own workload. With maps like these in hand, you can start to examine what creates smooth work-life rhythms and what interrupts or disrupts positive work-life dynamics. By mapping your day, you can notice when stress is building up and take action to reduce it. You can also build in more high point experiences, which will boost your resilience.

There are three specific small steps that will restore and sustain resilience: daily relaxation, detachment, and adequate sleep. Relaxation means physical relaxation, finding ways to unwind, release any tension, and allow your body to feel at ease. For some people, this may involve sitting or lying in a comfortable place that creates a sense of calm and rest. For others, physical exercise may be an important first step to release stress. I find walking to be very relaxing. Even though I am moving, walking helps me return to a calmer and more relaxed state. I sleep much better when I have been able to exercise or walk.

Detachment is time when you are not thinking about ministry or work, even in the back of your mind. Detaching activities focus your mind on something other than work, something that is in some way positive—peaceful, enjoyable, interesting, inspiring. These might include contemplative prayer, reading an engaging book, watching a television show you enjoy, or participating in a sport or other entertaining activity. While reading Scripture or other religious material is certainly important, be sure to select something that will not make you think about ministry. Detachment is time to engage your mind on something other than work.

Adequate sleep is the third resilience-boosting small step, although for some people (including me) getting enough sleep is not easy. Almost all of us need seven to nine hours of sleep each day. There are many books and internet resources that provide good advice about what we need to do to create better sleep. These include things like creating a regular sleep routine, engaging in calm and peaceful activities before bed, and limiting screen time before bed. I needed to work with my personal physician to create better sleep, and so I am on a prescribed regime of medication. While I would rather not take a pill to sleep, this is an important first small step for me. I am building in other small steps so that, in the future, the medication will no longer be necessary.

Look for something that will work for you. One resilient humanitarian worker I interviewed told me that he takes time every morning to journal about his life. It is his way of maintaining a good perspective on his work (by boosting self-awareness and self-reflectivity), and it helps him deal more effectively with work challenges (by increasing self-control). Another humanitarian worker takes a nap every day. He knows a nap will restore and reenergize him, so it is a priority except during emergencies. He tells his coworkers when it is nap time, and they honor that this wellbeing practice is important to him. Several physicians write poetry together because it helps them work through difficult issues from their medical practices. Poetry also helps them experience more joy in their practice of medicine. A number of Catholic and Protestant clergy use St. Ignatius's prayer of examination at the end of each day. They told us that this daily practice of reflection nourishes their spirits and helps them become better people and better pastors. These are just a few examples of how some caregivers sustain strong resilience capacities.

In addition to daily relaxation and detachment, each of us needs extended periods of relaxation and detachment. A real vacation is one in which you can truly take a break from your daily routines of work and life, taking time to relax, detach, and then restore yourself. This can be particular difficult for solo pastors who, although they may take time off from ministry, may nevertheless find themselves concerned about who is available in their absence to care for church members. Some churches have well-organized Stephen Ministries programs that, in addition to the excellent care they provide throughout the year, can provide high-quality care in the pastor's absence. Other times, pastors do not have the financial resources they need to truly "get away from it all," and gifts from individuals or organizations are needed to give them the opportunity for rest and restoration.

A final resilience booster is a somewhat larger step, but it offers the opportunity for an even greater boost to wellbeing: find your restorative niche. In the past we referred to these as hobbies, a term so often seen to mean an activity that is nice but unnecessary. A restorative niche can lead to significant increases in resilience, boost daily wellbeing, and increase the other dimensions of wellbeing, too. A restorative niche is something you really enjoy doing or find deeply meaningful that also requires skill and mastery. This combination creates flow experiences—moments in which we are fully engaged in a life-giving activity. During the flow of a restorative niche, we are fully absorbed because the activity takes our fullest efforts and because it is very positive experience. One of my restorative niches is backcountry hiking. An hour or two on the trail, pack on my back, and I am captivated by the beauty of God's world. I already mentioned that walking relaxes me, so hiking is a wonderful combination of wellbeing practices for me. One pastor I interviewed makes quilts, and that is her restorative niche. She donates the quilts, which boosts her wellbeing even more. Another pastor sings and plays music, all by himself. Lost in song he finds his "heart soars, his mind clears, and his spirit is lifted up." Still another pastor reads biographies and finds himself absorbed in the lives of people he admires. One of the most difficult challenges I found in taking this somewhat larger step was finding one of my restorative niches. I had to try several things until I finally tried hiking. I knew within a few hours it was the niche for me.

A WAY FORWARD FOR CHURCHES

Shortly after I began my research on flourishing in ministry, I was first exposed to the notion of a "pastor-killer" church, which I still find to be a sobering and distressful term. Unfortunately, it is an apt descriptor for the impact that some churches have on their pastors. In the section on a way forward for denominations, I urge leaders of religious organizations to take the reality of these churches seriously and to take concerted action to counter their destructive effects. Truly, some churches are life-depleting contexts that do serious damage to the health and wellbeing of their pastors.

Thankfully, there are pastor-nourishing churches on the opposite end of the spectrum that create life-enriching environments in which pastors flourish. These churches seek ways to help build and sustain the wellbeing of their pastors. Some pastor-nourishing churches assume a special role of being supportive and nurturing first appointments/first calls for new clergy. I have visited several of these churches and interviewed pastors who served at them. These are stories of the remarkable efforts of how local church members worked together to care for and support new pastors.

What can local churches do to foster the flourishing of clergy who serve them? First, they can use table 9.1 to help them develop initiatives and activities to support their pastors. A simple but profound example is to engage in intentional acts of gratitude toward the pastor (Bass 2018; Emmons 2008). A word of sincere thanks is one very powerful way we can boost the wellbeing of other people. There is an entire science that shows the power of gratitude, and local churches can harness this power to build and sustain the wellbeing of not just their pastors but also of the entire church community. Good thanksgiving is specific, personal, and genuine. "Great sermon today, pastor" will not do much. A description of something specific in the sermon and how it resonated or helped is more likely to be an effective positivity practice. Remembering that blanket "thanks" or a general "you're awesome" do not work well; there is no limit to the positive impact of the right kinds of gratitude. More thanks is almost always better. And giving thanks not only boosts the wellbeing of those we thank, but it also boosts our own wellbeing. The wise elders who encouraged us to say thank you to others and to count our blessings were right—it is an important spiritual practice and an important wellbeing practice.

Economic Sufficiency

A second and very key area for building and sustaining the wellbeing of clergy is to ensure pastors have the financial resources they need. The Lilly Endowment has supported a major grant initiative to over one hundred seminaries and regional and national denominational agencies to address the economic challenges facing pastors. Summarizing the discoveries that have emerged from these projects, Kirk Hadaway and Penny Long Marler (2017) identify these as particularly surprising and sobering:

- Denominational and congregational support are rarely mentioned as significant sources of financial support for seminary students.
- Inadequate retirement savings is a pervasive and urgent issue among clergy.
- Salary/compensation for clergy has historically (and appropriately) been modest; however, in aggregate, clergy compensation has diminished in recent decades compared to other identifiable occupations.
- The median income for clergy is $10,000 a year *less* than the median income for social workers or public school teachers.
- Financial stress is felt/reported most acutely among pastoral leaders who are women and pastors of color. They tend to receive lower salaries, fewer benefits, and have greater educational debt. On average, experienced female pastors and pastors of color earn 20 to 30 percent less than white, male pastors. This difference holds even after accounting for church size, years of experience, education, and other factors.
- Pastors serving in small congregations also often face significant financial challenges, and many of these pastors must find additional paid work or their spouse must work to be able to pay even for monthly living needs. Bivocationality is not always thrust upon pastors, but when it is, it creates additional life stressors.
- While pastoral leaders tend to express job satisfaction, a significant percentage have seriously considered leaving the ministry because of financial challenges/stress.

Jo Ann Deasy (2017), the director of institutional initiatives and student research at the Association of Theological Schools, reports that 54 percent of seminary students enter ministry with more than $37,000 of education debt, an amount that exceeds the starting pastoral salaries many of these students will receive.

Our research and studies of many other professions provide compelling evidence that financial challenges can be very detrimental to wellbeing. When financial resources are insufficient for meeting daily living needs, life is very challenging. Physical health is jeopardized. One pastor we interviewed ran out of money by the second week of the month and ate only rice until the next payday arrived. That is clearly not sufficient nutrition to sustain wellness. Stress levels increase dramatically as worries about making ends meet increase, and the pastor must spend more time on money-related matters instead of activities that boost wellbeing, such as spending time with family or engaging in ministry. The pain of misfortune is greater. Even a simple illness can be extremely burdensome when, for example, a pastor cannot pay to seek medical help or obtain necessary medication. And life is also more precarious. Paying for a flat tire or fixing a furnace can create of a cascade of financial shortfalls that may propel a pastor into severe financial distress. Many pastors are forgoing contributions to their Social Security funds so they can meet their current financial needs. This places their financial futures in grave peril. Unfortunately, pastors in poverty is a very real problem.

Churches do have many different and important ministries that need financial support. I would argue that few if any of these ministry needs are more important than ensuring the church's pastor and the pastor's family have sufficient, not just adequate, financial resources. Certainly being able to pay for monthly living needs is essential, but so is being able to plan for the future. Funds for emergencies, retirement planning, life insurance, and education planning for children are some of the important financial needs that clergy too often must forgo.

Hadaway, Marler, Deasy, and other experts note that pastors tend to internalize their financial challenges, often blaming themselves for making "poor choices" and suffering the negative effects in silence. The project leaders of Lilly's economic challenges grants report a pervasive sense of shame among the clergy who face financial difficulties. All of these experts agree that speaking with church leaders about their pay is difficult for many pastors. I urge church leaders to be proactive in addressing the financial needs of their pastors. Local church leaders can seek the support of projects within their denominational network that have received grants from Lilly's economic challenges initiative (see also www.firstfruitssummit.org). Many pension boards provide good help for dealing with clergy financial issues. And the resources I have included in the references section provide helpful information and a place for church leaders to begin.

Restoration and Renewal

A third way that local churches can support the flourishing of their pastors is to help clergy get adequate restoration and renewal. Restoration and renewal means time away from ministry responsibilities to rebuild resilience capacities, strengthen authenticity, and revitalize thriving. One essential is daily detachment from ministry. By detachment, I mean time in which the pastor can fully set aside any engagement with or thoughts about ministry work. This is time pastors can concentrate fully on important things other than ministry-related issues, especially time to give themselves fully to their family and friends and to self-care. I want to emphasize that detachment is much more than simply being away from the church facility. A growing body of research shows that, for many of us, the sight of our cell phones or computers causes us to think about work, even when we are at home. For pastors, proper detachment means not thinking about ministry-related matters for a period of time, so the cell phone and computer must be stored away, out of eyesight. When my wife was a pastor, she created a network of skilled church members who could staff the "care line," a phone number that members in need could call. This allowed her and the senior pastor to have detachment time because they knew emergencies would be taken care of well. Daily detachment is important—the goal should be that pastors can detach for at least an hour every day, including Sundays.

Helping pastors have a back stage is another high-impact way to foster restoration and renewal. For example, local churches can ensure pastors have time away from ministry and feel comfortable taking that time to gather with their back stage. Churches might provide other forms of backstage support, such as a small stipend for pastors who must travel to gather with their back stage or ensure that there is a private room in the church for the pastor to host backstage meetings.

In addition to daily detachment, pastors need time for extended detachment, time for a real vacation. Recent polls in the United States indicates that workers are accruing more unused vacation hours at the same time that most people are working more hours. Pastors often fit into this pattern as well. They are working more hours and taking less time for restoration and renewal. Remembering that detachment requires being able to set aside any thoughts about ministry, a real vacation is at least several days of continuous detachment. Taking a cell phone along means that the pastor will not have a truly restorative vacation. Leaving the area of the local church is also important to create the physical and psychological space for restoration and renewal to occur. This is an issue that a team of church members, working with the pastor and perhaps even other local churches, could address by creating new ideas about how they can ensure their pastors can experience restorative, renewing vacations. Financial stipends might also be important to ensure pastors can get away for a while.

A Community of Support

I left this part of the roadmap for local churches for last, in part because it may be the most important way that church leaders and members can support the flourishing of the pastors and the flourishing of the entire community of their local churches, by creating a circle of support around the pastor and the pastor's family. The chapters on social support and the stages of ministry provide more detail about what kinds of social support matter and why they matter. My encouragement here is for local church leaders and members to work together to create a community of social support. Church members working on their own to support pastors is important, but the strength of social support provided increases significantly when church members work together. For example, one pastor told of how she was greeted so warmly by members of the new church to which she had been appointed. On the day she and her family arrived, church members were waiting at their new house. In addition to a warm welcome, the members had put food in the kitchen for the first several days and provided a "welcome packet" with information about the town including local stores and restaurants; health-care providers; and a set of emergency numbers that included church members who could come to fix things, stay with the pastor's children, run errands, or help in any way they could. This was an auspicious beginning and began a very positive community of social support in which the pastor played a key role, but so did members of the church. Another pastor shared how his church "pounded him in" on his first day, each family bringing a pound (or a bit more) of important items: butter, sugar, detergent, cookies, blankets (it was winter), and even a "pound" of picture-hanging items so the pastor's family could make the house their home.

When pastors have provided us with examples of how church members created a community of support, they certainly described how church members responded when the pastor or the pastor's family faced a significant problem or crisis. We heard about church members who provided a special love offering to help the pastor meet financial challenges, members who loaned the pastor a car, and members who provided grief care when the pastor experienced the death of a loved one. Equally important were the more prosaic, everyday stories—handwritten notes of thanks, church members who took it upon themselves to be responsible for church tasks (like cleaning the sanctuary after Sunday services or mowing the church lawn), and those who actively participated in church ministries.

Among the actions that pastors seemed to cherish most were when church members affirmed the pastor's leadership and ministry. Sincere affirmations from the people the pastor has been called to serve and lead are immensely impactful forms of social support. The absence of such affirmations can leave pastors in limbo, wondering whether they are serving and leading the church well, so intentional acts of affirmation are a powerful way for churches to create a community of support. Likewise, while some critical feedback may be necessary, delivering that feedback in a beneficent way is important for pastors, as it is for all of us. Years ago a pastor said that sometimes pastoral ministry can feel like "death by a thousand paper cuts."

He was referring to the small complaints, veiled criticisms, and congregational nit-picking that pastors may experience from church members. Harsh criticisms or complaints are rarely effective and never necessary. Any concern can and should be framed in a way that leads to productive conversation. I think it is the church's responsibility to respond to members who are being unduly critical or outright hostile to the pastor. Certainly the pastor may also have a role in responding to the actions of such members, but other members also have the right and I think also the responsibility for creating the best community of support for the pastor and the church. There have been times that I have ignored or tolerated the unkind actions other church members directed toward the pastors of the churches I attended. And there was also a time when a church member very appropriately admonished me on a better way to share my concerns with the pastor. Those experiences, and the research my team and I have conducted, have confirmed for me the importance of being an active participant in creating a community of support around the pastor. In the end, creating strong social support for the pastor and the pastor's family will also lead to a richer community for all church members.

ROADMAP FOR DENOMINATIONS

Religious organizations, whether denominations or the informal networks created among independent churches, have a powerful but subtle and often overlooked impact on clergy wellbeing. I want to highlight two ways that denominational systems impact clergy wellbeing: processes for ordination and credentialing and for appointing or calling pastors to local churches. In this section I describe how these processes are important, especially because they establish, early in a pastor's ministry, expectations about who pastors should be and how pastors should act. I discuss how ordination processes and interactions with credentialing boards are a critical first step toward a trajectory of either wellbeing or ill-being. I then describe how systems for appointing or calling pastors often overlook factors that play a central role in both a pastor's future success and wellbeing in a particular ministry context. I return to some of the themes of chapter 4, but here I describe how both appointment and call systems can incorporate our findings to create better pastor-church matches and, in turn, how those better matches lead to greater effectiveness in ministry and higher clergy wellbeing. I end the chapter by sharing research findings on elements of denominational cultures. I focus in particular on deeply held norms about being a pastor. For example, whether norms about pastors are gendered—good pastors are strong leaders, pastors should be decisive and commanding, good pastors are charismatic—and present particular challenges for women in ministry. I discuss how the changing nature of religious practice is creating tensions with traditional norms about being a pastor and also how younger clergy respond to traditional norms.

Before I turn to the ways denominations can support wellbeing, I want to begin with perhaps the most important way denominations can support clergy wellbeing, and that is by responding effectively to the mistreatment of clergy by local church members. In our Flourishing in Ministry research, we have heard stories from pastors that detail mistreatment, hostility, and even abuse by members of local churches. These stories portray that pastors often do not feel they have the power or clout to address these problems on their own, in part because their financial livelihoods and futures in ministry are often at stake in such situations. Young pastors, female clergy, and pastors of color are much more likely to be targets of mistreatment and much less likely to have adequate support to respond on their own. This is an area in which larger judicatory and denominational systems can, and I would argue should, take action. Many of these systems are responding, and I commend these organizations for taking the lead in addressing this important area of need. Because organizations of all kinds are finally addressing issues of sexual harassment and other forms of abuse, best practices have been established for the kinds of formal systems that will work best for ensuring clergy can seek and get help dealing with mistreatment. Third-party involvement is often necessary to ensure incidents of mistreatment are reported. This system could provide additional resources to help clergy deal more effectively with their local churches in areas such as conflict management and negotiation. Again, this is an issue in which denominations and judicatories can make decisive and important impacts on clergy wellbeing.

Pastoral Credentialing

Most denominations have a formal process that candidates follow as they journey from sensing a call to ministry to receiving full pastoral ordination. Whether the process is governed by a denominational policy or a local church, this process is typically described as having two principle phases or steps. The first phase is to help candidates discern and confirm their call to ministry. Here candidates are usually guided or shepherded by someone who can help them clarify their sense of calling, test the spiritual foundations of that calling—is it a call from God or wishful thinking?—and ensure that it is a call is to pastoral ministry and not a call to another form of service. The second phase is, having confirmed a vocational call, to ensure a candidate is properly equipped for ministry by possessing the necessary educational training, personal characteristics, and spiritual formation to become an ordained or credentialed pastor. Often a considerable amount of time may pass between these two phases, as candidates whose call has been confirmed engage in educational and pastoral formation through seminary, on-the-job training, or some combination of both. This second phase ends in ordination or some other formal conferral that the candidate has become a pastor. Both of these phases are important for ensuring what I referred to in chapter 3 as professional legitimacy.

Another outcome of the credentialing process is the way it shapes a candidate's pastoral identity. As I described in chapter 7, candidates have to find a way to achieve both legitimacy as a pastor—to aspire to and meet the standards that all pastors must achieve—and find a way to be authentic as a pastor. Credentialing processes impact whether pastors can achieve authenticity. These processes convey, in powerful albeit implicit ways, norms about the pastorate. These norms set expectations not only about what pastors are supposed to do but also about what it means to be a pastor and even who can truly be a pastor. Credentialing processes can create clear but also flexible pathways in which pastors can achieve both authenticity and professional legitimacy. Sometimes, however, credentialing processes create strong identity demands that constrain pastors' abilities to achieve authenticity. We heard stories, for example, about how pastors felt compelled to express certain dogmas to gain approval from credentialing boards. One pastor explained how he and other candidates felt: "I mean, we were tested to the extreme. We felt that they were trying to make us into [copies of them], and so we were all trying to figure out how to be as honest as we could but also avoid getting trapped into espousing a view we did not agree with." Certainly denominations do have a set of core beliefs that are regarded as essential, and pastors are rightly expected to affirm and embrace those beliefs. Adherence to such beliefs does not create identity demands, especially when those core beliefs are clearly defined and well understood across the denomination. Credentialing processes become problematic when they create identity demands that pressure candidates to conform in ways that unduly constrain their capacities to be authentic. When pastors seek to conform to identity demands, they are trying to stuff the round peg of their true selves into the square hole of the identity demands. Over time, these attempts at conformance can leave pastors with poorly formed or even fragmented pastoral identities.

Again here, we found that women and pastors of color who were members of predominantly white denominations were more likely to experience identity demands during the credentialing process. Younger pastors may be more likely to internalize these expectations because they are still developing true self-knowledge and self-integrity.

The key is for the credentialing process to ensure professional legitimacy and also facilitate the development of an authentic pastoral identity. Sometimes this can feel, as one member of a credentialing board put it, "like threading a camel through the eye of a needle." It is more than just trying to balance legitimacy and authenticity. There is an art to creating both clear and firm standards that all candidates must meet and also creating enough space for candidates to express these standards in their own unique and authentic ways. But in my judgment, if those people who lead and facilitate these processes aspire to achieving both, that alone will make a positive difference.

Facilitating Better Pastor-Church Alignment

Another very important and often overworked group is persons engaged in matching pastors with local churches. Whether this is done by a judicatory group or members of a local church, the people involved are almost certainly adding this to other work and life commitments. Yet they know it is one of the most important decisions for the life the local church, the pastor and pastor's family, and the denomination. In addition, it is very uncommon that these people have a background in human resource management, so they are operating at their best in what for them is unknown and uncertain territory. Even with all of these challenges, any time I have had the opportunity to watch these decisions unfold, I am impressed with the care, diligence, and sincerity that people bring to this process. And I find that people who make these decisions are eager for ways they can do their work better. I think there are two fairly simple and straightforward things that will help ensure that appointment or call decisions create matches that are good for pastors and local churches.

The first builds on research insights on authenticity from chapter 3. I wrote there about the importance of true self-knowledge, knowing our strengths and weakness, the better angels of our nature and our brokenness. One way to facilitate good pastor-church alignment is for pastors to be comfortable sharing true self-knowledge about their pastoral identities. Pastors should share their visions for ministry and why they feel called by God to the pastorate. They should be able to share what ministry activities they can do well and what they cannot do. They need to share their ministry preferences, including what they like to do and what they dislike doing. And ideally they need to share their ministry weaknesses. By weaknesses I do not mean strengths masquerading as weaknesses—like "Sometimes my aspirations to be the best pastor cause me to spend more time on sermon preparation than perhaps would be ideal." That will not help. Nor am I suggesting that pastors need to share traumas or personal challenges. This is not about sharing deep secrets or laying bare one's soul. I am encouraging pastors to share true self-knowledge that is directly relevant to the kind of pastor they are and can be for this new church, for example, a tendency to worry about preaching or feeling uncomfortable doing hospital visits.

Churches and church leaders should do the same. Churches must make a careful and candid accounting of their ministry strengths and weaknesses, likes and dislikes, and the glorious and uncomfortable aspects of the church's history or culture. Church leaders should share similarly true self-knowledge of themselves. I recommend that sharing begins with true knowledge of the church that the leaders and pastor-candidate share together. Church members should share true knowledge about the church first to create an open and safe environment for church leaders and the pastor-candidate to share about themselves. Mutual pledges to maintain strict confidentiality would also help create space for candid sharing.

In congregation-based polities, this can all fit into the customary processes that are in place. In episcopal, hierarchical, or connexional polities, judicatories can adapt current processes to facilitate this mutual sharing of true knowledge.

The second way to improve pastor–local church alignment will take place after the selection of a new pastor has been confirmed. Church leaders and the pastor should meet as soon as feasible and map out roles and responsibilities of the pastor, lay leaders, and church members. This mapping of roles and responsibilities will build off of the open and candid sharing of strengths and weaknesses. The goal in this mapping process is to establish clarity about what falls under the pastor's role and what falls to lay leaders and other members. This mapping should cover daily ministry activities, regular worship services, and any regular or special events the church hosts. My sense is that few churches and pastors have established enough clarity about roles and responsibilities.

Especially important is open and candid sharing about fundamental beliefs and how they shape ministry vision. By fundamental beliefs I mean what in chapter 4 I referred to as core life values and beliefs—for both pastor and church, being clear about the most important beliefs and values that shape their understanding of Christian faith and the role of the church in the world. We heard stories from a number of pastors about the central importance of missiology—reaching out to serve and connect with people beyond the members of the local church—for their calling and their foundational understanding of the role local churches are supposed to fill in the world. These pastors described their church members as more inward focused and therefore emphasizing church ministries and activities that predominantly served members. These pastors spoke with respect of their church's ministries but also about a fundamental disconnect they felt between what they saw as important and what members of the church saw as important. The process I am advocating here is surfacing these issues at the very beginning, when a pastor is just entering into the leadership role at the new church. This involves more than seeking agreement on a church mission statement, as important as that is. It requires being clear about the fundamental beliefs and values that shape that mission statement. When pastors spoke about getting "buy-in" from church members on a mission statement or on major church initiatives, buy-in almost always meant a deeper consensus about the fundamental beliefs and values, why they matter, and how they shape the ministries and activities of the church.

Denomination leaders do care about pastors, and they care about their local churches. Leaders want their pastors to flourish, and they want their churches to flourish. My hope is that these three roadmaps can be used together to help pastors, church leaders and members, and denominational leaders as they aspire to foster flourishing clergy and a flourishing community of churches.

References

Avolio, Bruce J., Fred O. Walumbwa, and Todd J. Weber. 2009. "Leadership: Current Theories, Research, and Future Directions." *Annual Review of Psychology* 60 (1): 421–49.

Adams, C. J., H. Hough, R. J. Proeschold-Bell et al. 2007. "Clergy Burnout: A Comparison Study with Other Helping Professions." *Pastoral Psychology* 66: 147–75.

Bai, Yang, Laura A. Maruskin, Serena Chen, Amie M. Gordon, Jennifer E. Stellar, Galen D. McNeil, Kaiping Peng, and Dacher Keltner. 2017. "Awe, the Diminished Self, and Collective Engagement: Universals and Cultural Variations in the Small Self." *Journal of Personality and Social Psychology* 113 (2): 185–209.

Bass, Diana Butler. 2018. *Grateful: The Transformative Power of Giving Thanks.* New York: HarperCollins.

Baumeister, Roy F. 1991. *Meanings of Life.* New York: Guilford Press.

Baumeister, Roy F., and Mark R. Leary. 1995. "The Need to Belong: Desire for Interpersonal Attachments as a Fundamental Human Motivation." *Psychological Bulletin* 117 (3): 497–529.

Baumeister, Roy F., and John Tierney. 2011. *Willpower: Rediscovering the Greatest Human Strength.* New York: Penguin Press.

Berscheid, Elaine. 2010. "Love in the Fourth Dimension." *Annual Review of Psychology* 61 (1): 1–25.

Bloom, Matt. 2013. *Emerging Research Insights on the Well-Being of Pastors.* https://workwellresearch.com/media/images/Emerging%20Insights.pdf. Accessed June 1, 2018.

Cacioppo, John T., and William Patrick. 2009. *Loneliness: Human Nature and the Need for Social Connection.* New York: Norton.

Carroll, Jackson W. 2006. *God's Potters: Pastoral Leadership and the Shaping of Congregations.* Grand Rapids, MI: William B. Eerdmans.

Clapper, Gregory Scott. 2011. *The Renewal of the Heart Is the Mission of the Church: Wesley's Heart Religion in the Twenty-First Century.* Cambridge, UK: Lutterworth Press.

Clark, Margaret S. 2018. "What Is Good and What Is Missing in Relationship Theory and Research." In *The Cambridge Handbook of Personal Relationships*, second edition, 28–38. Cambridge: Cambridge University Press.

Cohen, Geoffrey L., and David K. Sherman. 2014. "The Psychology of Change: Self-Affirmation and Social Psychological Intervention." *Annual Review of Psychology* 65 (1): 333–71.

Crocker, Jennifer, and Connie T. Wolfe. 2001. "Contingencies of Self-Worth." *Psychological Review* 108 (3): 593–623.

Daniel, Lillian, and Martin B. Copenhaver. 2009. *This Odd and Wondrous Calling: The Public and Private Lives of Two Ministers.* Grand Rapids, MI: William B. Eerdmans.

Davis, Don E., and Joshua A. Hicks. 2013. "Maintaining Hope at the 11th Hour: Authenticity Buffers the Effect of Limited Time Perspective on Hope." *Personality and Social Psychology Bulletin* 39 (12): 1634–46.

Deasy, Jo Ann. 2017. "Virtuous Cycles: Supporting Future Ministers." *Reflections: A Magazine of Theological and Ethical Inquiry from Yale Divinity School.* https://reflections.yale.edu/article/god-and-money-turning-tables/virtuous-cycles-supporting-future-ministers. Accessed January 22, 2019.

DeShon, Richard P. 2010. "Clergy Effectiveness: National Survey Results." Nashville, TN: General Board of Higher Education and Ministry of the United Methodist Church.

DeShon, Richard P., and Abigail Quinn. 2007. "Job Analysis Generalizability Study for the Position of United Methodist Local Pastor." General Board of Higher Education and Ministry, United Methodist Church, 20.

Diamond, Adele. 2013. "Executive Functions." *Annual Review of Psychology* 64 (1): 135–68.

Diener, Ed, and Robert Biswas-Diener. 2011. *Happiness: Unlocking the Mysteries of Psychological Wealth.* Malden, MA: Blackwell.

Emmons, Robert A. 2008. *Thanks! How Practicing Gratitude Can Make You Happier.* New York: Houghton Mifflin.

Fiske, Susan T. 2011. *Envy Up, Scorn Down: How Status Divides Us.* New York: Russell Sage Foundation.

Fredrickson, Barbara L. 2004. "What Good Are Positive Emotions?" *Review of General Psychology: Journal of Division 1, of the American Psychological Association* 2 (3): 1–20.

Fredrickson, Barbara L., and Marcial F. Losada. 2005. "Positive Affect and the Complex Dynamics of Human Flourishing." *American Psychologist* 60 (7): 678–86.

Friedman, Edwin H. 2007. *A Failure of Nerve: Leadership in the Age of the Quick Fix.* Edited by Margaret M. Treadwell and Edward W. Beal. New York: Seabury Books.

Gerber, J. P., Ladd Wheeler, and Jerry Suls. 2018. "A Social Comparison Theory Meta-Analysis 60+ Years On." *Psychological Bulletin* 144 (2): 177–97.

Goffman, Erving. 1956. *The Presentation of Self in Everyday Life.* New York: Doubleday.

Gottman, John, and Nan Silver. 2014. *What Makes Love Last? How to Build Trust and Avoid Betrayal.* New York: Simon and Schuster.

Hadaway, C. Kirk, and Penny Long Marler. 2017. "Economic Challenges Facing Pastoral Leaders: Report on NEI Planning Grant Research 2015–2016." Report to the Lilly Endowment, Inc. http://ecfpl.org/wp-content/uploads/2019/01/ECFPL-Hadaway-Marler-Research-Report.pdf. Accessed January 22, 2019.

Harter, Susan. 2002. "Authenticity." In *Handbook of Positive Psychology,* edited by Chris R. Snyder and Shane J. Lopez, 382–94. Oxford: Oxford University Press.

Hawkley, Louise C., and John T. Cacioppo. 2010. "Loneliness Matters: A Theoretical and Empirical Review of Consequences and Mechanisms." *Annals of Behavioral Medicine* 40 (2): 218–27.

Heifetz, Ronald, Alexander Grashow, and Marty Linsky. 2009. *The Practice of Adaptive Leadership: Tools and Tactics for Changing Your Organization and the World.* Boston: Harvard Business Press.

Hewlin, Patricia F. 2009. "Wearing the Cloak: Antecedents and Consequences of Creating Facades of Conformity." *Journal of Applied Psychology* 94 (3): 727–41.

Jordan, Christian H., Steven J. Spencer, Mark P. Zanna, Etsuko Hoshino-Browne, and Joshua Correll. 2003. "Secure and Defensive High Self-Esteem." *Journal of Personality and Social Psychology* 85 (5): 969–78.

Kahneman, Daniel, Ed Diener, and Norbert Schwarz. 2003. *Well-Being: The Foundations of Hedonic Psychology.* New York: Russell Sage Foundation.

Kernis, Michael H. 2005. "Measuring Self-Esteem in Context: The Importance of Stability of Self-Esteem in Psychological Functioning." *Journal of Personality* 73 (6): 1569–1605.

Kernis, Michael H., and Brian M. Goldman. 2006. "A Multicomponent Conceptualization of Authenticity: Theory and Research." *Advances in Experimental Social Psychology* 38: 283–357.

Kraut, Robert, Michael Patterson, Vicki Lundmark, Sara Kiesler, Tridas Mukopadhyay, and William Scherlis. 1998. "Internet Paradox: A Social Technology That Reduces Social Involvement and Psychological Well-Being?" *American Psychologist* 53 (9): 1017–31.

Lyubomirsky, Sonja. 2008. *The How of Happiness: A New Approach to Getting the Life You Want*. New York: Penguin Books.

Lyubomirsky, Sonja, Laura A. King, and Ed Diener. 2005. "The Benefits of Frequent Positive Affect: Does Happiness Lead to Success?" *Psychological Bulletin* 131 (6): 803–55.

Markman, Keith D., Travis Proulx, and Matthew J. Lindberg. 2013. *The Psychology of Meaning*. Washington, DC: American Psychological Association.

McAdams, Dan P. 2013. *The Redemptive Self: Stories Americans Live By*. New York: Oxford University Press.

McMahon, Darrin. 2005. *Happiness: A History*. New York: Atlantic Monthly Press.

Miller, Earl K. 2017. "Multitasking: Why Your Brain Can't Do It and What You Should Do about It." Massachusetts Institute of Technology. https://radius.mit.edu/sites/default/files/images/Miller%20Multitasking%202017.pdf. Accessed June 1, 2018.

Neuhaus, Richard John. 1992. *Freedom for Ministry*. Grand Rapids, MI: William B. Eerdmans.

Oates, Wayne Edward. 1982. *The Christian Pastor*. Philadelphia: Westminster Press.

Ophir, Eyal, Clifford Nass, and Anthony D. Wagner. 2009. "Cognitive Control in Media Multitaskers." *Proceedings of the National Academy of Sciences of the United States of America* 106 (37): 15583–87.

Pallini, Susana, Antonio Chirumbolo, Mara Morelli, Roberto Baiocco, Fiorenzo Laghi, and Nancy Eisenberg. 2018. "The Relation of Attachment Security Status to Effortful Self-Regulation: A Meta-Analysis." *Psychological Bulletin* 144 (5): 501–31.

Peterson, Eugene. 2011. *The Pastor: A Memoir*. New York: HarperCollins.

Pew Forums. 2016. "Choosing a New Church or House of Worship." http://www.pewforum.org/2016/08/23/choosing-a-new-church-or-house-of-worship/. Accessed February 21, 2019.

Pressman, Sarah D., and Sherman Cohen. 2005. "Does Positive Affect Influence Health?" *Psychological Bulletin* 131 (6): 925–71.

Rudd, Melanie, Katherine D. Vohs, and Jennifer Aaker. 2012. "Awe Expands People's Perception of Time, Alters Decision Making, and Enhances Well-Being." *Psychological Science* 23 (10): 1130–36.

Ryff, Carol D., and Corey L. M. Keyes. 1995. "The Structure of Psychological Well-Being Revisited." *Journal of Personality and Social Psychology* 69 (4): 719.

Seligman, Martin E. P. 2013. *Flourish: A Visionary New Understanding of Happiness and Well-Being*. New York: Atria.

Stellar, Jennifer E., Amie Gordon, Craig L. Anderson, Paul K. Piff, Galen D. McNeil, and Dacher Keltner. 2018. "Awe and Humility." *Journal of Personality and Social Psychology* 114 (2): 258–69.

Sullivan, William M. 2005. *Work and Integrity: The Crisis and Promise of Professionalism in America*. San Francisco: Jossey-Bass.

This I Believe. https://www.npr.org/series/4538138/this-i-believe. Accessed May 14, 2019.

Thoits, Peggy A. 2011. "Mechanisms Linking Social Ties and Support to Physical and Mental Health." *Journal of Health and Social Behavior* 52 (2): 145–61.

Vaillant, George Eman. 2002. *Aging Well: Surprising Guideposts to a Happier Life from the Landmark Harvard Study of Adult Development*. Boston: Little, Brown and Co.

Waterman, Alan S. 2015. *Best within Us: Positive Psychology Perspectives on Eudaimonia*. Washington, DC: American Psychological Association.

Wayment, Heidi A., and Jack J. Bauer. 2008. *Transcending Self-Interest: Psychological Explorations of the Quiet Ego*. Washington, DC: American Psychological Association.

Williams, Joan C., Jennifer L. Berdahl, and Joseph A. Vandello. 2016. "Beyond Work-Life 'Integration.'" *Annual Review of Psychology* 67 (1): 515–39.

Williams, Kipling D. 2007. "Ostracism." *Annual Review of Psychology* 58 (1): 425–52.

Williams, Kipling D., and Steven A. Nida. 2011. "Ostracism: Consequences and Coping." *Current Directions in Pscyhological Science* 20 (2): 71–75.

Yale Center for Faith and Culture. 2011. "Consultation of Happiness and Human Flourishing." https://faith.yale.edu/god-human-flourishing/happiness-and-human-flourishing.   Accessed February 21, 2019.

Index

About the Author

Matt Bloom has been a professor at the Mendoza College of Business at the University of Notre Dame since 1996. He teaches classes to graduate students and organizational leaders on innovation and design thinking. Since 2009 he has led the Wellbeing at Work Program, which includes the Flourishing in Ministry project. Matt splits his time between South Bend, Indiana, and Washington, DC. Matt is married to Kim. Matt's son Nicholas is a design consultant in Washington, DC. His son Keaton is an architect. Keaton and his wife, Maíra Fonseca, a dermatologist, live in Manhattan, New York.

To learn more about Flourishing in Ministry research, including gaining access to our online wellbeing assessment and our mobile application, please visit our project website at www.flourishinginministry.org.